Attract The Love
You Deserve

First published as *Atrae el amor que te mereces* in 2022 by Zenith,
an imprint of Editorial Planeta

© Editorial Planeta, S.A 2022
Zenith is an imprint of Editorial Planeta, S.A. Avda. Diagonal 662-664, 08034 Barcelona (Spain)

This English-language hardback edition first published in 2023 by Quadrille,
an imprint of Hardie Grant Publishing

Quadrille
52–54 Southwark Street
London SE1 1UN
quadrille.com

For the English-language hardback edition:
Managing Director Sarah Lavelle
Project Editor Sofie Shearman
Translator Lauren Voaden
Cover Design Katy Everett
Interior Design and Layout The Social Vim Collective
Illustrations The Social Vim Collective, Shutterstock
Head of Production Stephen Lang
Production Controller Katie Jarvis

Cataloguing in Publication Data:
a catalogue record for this book
is available from the British Library.

ISBN 978 1 83783 032 9

Printed in China

Sara Gomar
@astro_realizacion

Attract The Love
You Deserve

An Astrological Guide
to Empowered Relationships

Translated by Lauren Voaden

Hardie Grant

QUADRILLE

Contents

*To my mum, for ingraining her
way of seeing the world into me.
To my grandmother and my
kitten, the purest and most beautiful
beings I've ever known.
To the great women and men who
have brightened my path.
To the universe.*

Foreword

Never go in search of love; go in search of life, and life will find you the love you seek.
ATTICUS

When I started writing this book, I'd just entered a new romantic relationship. I'd been single for a long time, and I was somewhat apprehensive about embarking on a new romantic adventure. My previous relationships had been a total disaster, and I spent a long time protecting myself so that I didn't end up reliving the same painful situations. I'd become used to being alone; I'd made my peace with it and wasn't particularly interested in finding a partner. But, when you meet that special someone, the inevitable cascade of emotions ensues and before you know it, you're in love again. As much as we say that we're better off alone – that we don't need anyone – we somehow can't seem to avoid temptation when we meet someone and fall in love. We all *love* love. That magical feeling that appears out of nowhere and turns our world upside down. Finding the one, our special person out of all the people we meet every day, remains one of life's great mysteries.

Sometimes I wonder what strange force comes between two people who, without knowing each other at all, just so happen to find themselves in the same place at the same time and are irremediably attracted to one another. One day, out of nowhere, this connection appears and changes your life completely, illuminating everything and filling it with new meaning. Romantic love is powerful. It could be labelled 'poison', and yet we'd drink it anyway. No one escapes its spell. No one is immune to its magnetic attraction. We're born with this innate desire, as if it were a chip that had been implanted into each and every one of us. Although the desire might subside over the years, our hearts will always yearn for it, as if our lives are lacking something that prevents us from feeling complete. When two people meet, it creates a new energy that didn't exist before, and through that interaction a transformation takes place. You both create the relationship, and the relationship creates you.

For the universe, there's no such thing as chance. Every meaningful romantic encounter conceals a deeper meaning that transcends our understanding. Love isn't about requests or demands, nor is it about chasing a fantasy or fulfilling expectations. It's not about possessing or moulding the other to our liking. Love isn't there to meet our needs, take care of us or fill our emptiness. It exists so that you can discover yourself through another, so that you can take a leap of consciousness, learning and growing with every step. It's about allowing the other to evolve as they travel their own path, regardless of whether that leads them away from you.

Love fascinates us, and when a new love story appears on the horizon, we feel a combination of anxiety and curiosity, which leads us towards that person who drives us crazy. I admit that these romantic doubts – which don't seem very deep at first glance – were the reason I first approached astrology when I was a teenager.

I've always had an interest in the magical and the occult. My entire life, I've nurtured a curiosity to find out why we're here and what the purpose of everything is. Perhaps because I'm a Libra rising, my search for love has occupied a lot of space in my life and led me to write a book about relationships. Over the years, I discovered that astrology is a tool with a potential that goes far beyond wanting to know the future of a relationship or how compatible two people might be. It's a powerful guide to self-understanding, a unique and exclusive roadmap of yourself. Your birth chart seems to say that everything happens for a profound reason. Every challenge you face is designed to return your power to you. It's not about understanding the person in front of you or knowing which way things will go: it's about you, because what you're like as an individual will affect the type of relationship you have.

Astrology helps you understand that what you are and how your life unfolds are not unrelated. It's true that we're living in hostile times for relationships; it seems the old conventions haven't adapted to the new age, and we're in a period of transition in which we're finding new ways of bonding. The rise of social media and apps; the intense desire to experience new things; the appearance-based culture; big cities; fast-paced lives: these things aren't conducive to lasting, satisfying love. We're putting up with less and less, and there are many disappointments that reveal how hard it is to keep the flame of love alive.

Of all the bonds that we freely establish throughout our lives, romantic relationships are capable of stirring intense emotions and dark passions that would otherwise remain dormant. Every one of of us experiences love differently. We each feel differently and all have a particular way of perceiving emotional security and experiencing sexuality. Add all this to the events we've experienced throughout our lives and the wounds we carry, and everything becomes very complex. Instead of working to build something solid, we've become accustomed to instantaneity and giving up at the slightest hurdle – especially when the initial thrill and delight of the first few months is over. As soon as things get difficult, we jump from one relationship to the next, instead of trying to understand what's going on. We can change our partner, but if we don't work on our own personal development, we'll keep reliving the same situations over and over again. We know that nothing lasts forever, but why does the magic end so quickly? What prevents us from understanding our differences and working to transform those obstacles into more love?

I've written the book that I would have liked to have found years ago, and I'm convinced that reading it would have saved me a lot of unnecessary suffering. The purpose of this book is to shed some light on the role you play in everything that happens to you and the extent to which you're able to change the circumstances you find yourself in. In order to enjoy fuller and more mindful relationships, it's vital that you better your self-understanding and increase the possibilities open to you; only then will you be able to attract the love that you deserve. The key is within you – nowhere else. Never forget the power you possess.

CHAPTER 1

Venus

Love and the
female essence

♀

VENUS

There is no greater power than that of the sun, the moon, and a woman who knows her worth.

NICOLE LYONS

Venus is the ultimate embodiment of femininity. This planet represents the things we like, the things we find beautiful and the things we value. Though it's known as the planet of love, beauty and relationships, its meaning extends much deeper. In ancient times, Venus was regarded as a powerful element of feminine energy and was associated with the power of nature and the creation of life. Venus and Earth are considered twin planets, being almost identical in size, mass and volume. Some recent studies suggest that millions of years ago, when the universe was still very young, Venus enjoyed a temperate climate with blue skies and plenty of water forming rivers and oceans on its surface. However, over time the two planets seemed to switch places, with Earth now enjoying mild conditions while Venus has become a true hellscape with inhospitable scorching temperatures. It's as if these planets share a connection deeper than we can possibly comprehend. Venus is a mysterious planet with incredible symbolic influence, and there's a lot to be learned from studying its cycles and the myths that surround it. It's one of the brightest celestial bodies in the night sky, second only to the Moon. This beautiful light that our ancestors would have gazed upon is also visible during the daytime, so it's no coincidence that it became associated with beauty in all its many forms. Without the powerful telescopes we have today, our ancestors would have observed its cycles with nothing but the naked eye, creating myths and legends to explain its influence on physical reality. Studying its movement across the celestial sphere helps us understand the planet beyond its practical interpretation, which we'll explore in depth in the following pages.

THE VENUS CYCLE:
THE MORNING AND EVENING STAR

Historically, no astrological event has been as observed, feared and admired as the cycles between Venus, the Sun and the Earth. These cycles have even been linked to the mysteries surrounding the creation of life itself. Numerous civilizations worshipped Venus and even synchronized their calendars with its cycles. For the Mayans, the planet's movement was central to their measurement of time, and they recorded it with incredible precision. The synodic cycle of Venus (the time it takes for the planet to reappear at the same point in the sky with respect to the Sun) is 584 days long and begins with an inferior conjunction between Venus and the Sun. We refer to planetary conjunction when two or more planets are close together in the sky, usually in the same sign. It's the most powerful alignment because the planets' energies merge and act in unison. In the synodic cycle, Venus, the planet of love, is placed between the Earth and the Sun in an event similar to an eclipse (when the Moon comes between the Earth and the Sun), only Venus is smaller and cannot totally block it out. This conjunction occurs when Venus is at the midpoint of its retrograde cycle (from the Earth it appears to be heading backwards rather than forwards) and is moving very slowly through the Zodiac. At this time, Venus is at its closest point to the Earth and is called the Morning Star. In ancient times, it had initiatory and mystical connotations, representing the triumph of the goddess over darkness. It's a time of rebirth and new beginnings, equivalent to the new moon phase of the lunar cycle, in which we leave behind all that is useless to start a completely new cycle. Eight days later, we can see Venus on the horizon at dawn, before sunrise.

Nine months later, already in direct motion, our goddess will reach its maximum speed (one degree and fifteen minutes per day) and will join the Sun again, this time in superior conjunction. On this occasion, the Sun is positioned between Earth and Venus from a terrestrial viewpoint. The planet of love is then at its farthest point from the Earth and is equivalent to the opposition aspect of the full moon phase of the lunar cycle. It represents a moment of culmination, a flowering, in which we reach an understanding of the themes associated with the planet. At this time it's called the Evening Star, and a few days later we can see it in the night sky at sunset.

THE PENTAGRAM OF VENUS

Every eight years, Venus' orbit forms a perfect geometric rose or pentagram as it dances with the Earth. During this period, five inferior and five superior conjunctions take place, which combine to create this beautiful image that reflects the beauty and harmony of the cosmos. This sacred pattern magically symbolizes the essence of the planet: love, beauty and femininity. It represents the beauty that has been widely applied in art and architecture. Historically, philosophical viewpoints considered Venus not just to be the goddess of love, but the soul of the world and the basis of all life. It's no coincidence that these conjunctions are separated into nine-month periods, coinciding in a wonderful way with the time we spend growing in the womb. Today we can consider Venus a key planet for increasing our vibration and with it, that of the Earth. The magical moment when Venus and the Sun meet is called Venus Star Point in astrology, a modern concept coined by astrologer Arielle Guttman. If we mark this point, we can observe that Venus' sacred journey around the Sun draws a pentagram.

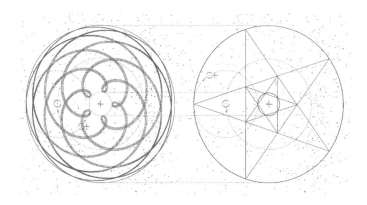

The pentagram was a pre-Christian pagan symbol associated with nature worship. For women in ancient times who practised natural magic, each point of the star represented one of the four elements (fire, earth, air and water), and the point that pointed towards the sky was the ether or spirit. This sacred symbol was intrinsically connected to feminine divinity and the power of the goddess, and it has always been regarded as a symbol of perfection, light and the pursuit of wisdom. This remained true until the arrival of the Middle Ages and the Spanish Inquisition, when the symbol's association with the occult and witch-craft was distorted. The pentagram and its link to the sacred number five has roots in many ancient and contemporary cultures spanning East and West. In Hinduism, the god Shiva is depicted as having five faces. Traditional Eastern medicine is also based on the "five elements", and the alchemists were looking for the "quintessence", the element that would enable them to produce the philosophers' stone. The Pythagoreans considered it to be a way to access mysterious and profound knowledge. It's also represented in the Tarot in the minor arcana of gold. The circles of Venus' orbit also resemble a rose, which was a sacred symbol in the West. This magical flower signifies perfec-tion, achievement and mystery, and is another symbol associated with the planet since its beauty and fragrance symbolize love, and its thorns symbolize the wounds that love can cause. The rose is related to the heart as the centre of consciousness and spirit. The enlightened heart that has achieved purity of being was represented as a rose with open petals. The shape of the flower's calyx resembles a receptacle, which is why it's associated with the Holy Grail, which is not a physical object, but rather the essence of the goddess (feminine energy) that returns to restore balance to humanity.

The energy of Venus was also associated with apples, which in many myths were considered the fruit of life. If you cut an apple in half crosswise, you'll see its seed cavity forms a pentagram, making it a magical fruit. They are a symbol of love, youth, beauty and knowledge. In fact, there are many love spells and rituals that take advantage of the magical power of this fruit and the pentagram it contains. The golden apple is an element that appears in legends and fairy tales in many countries. It can symbolize eternal youth, immortality or rebirth. It's also related to the Garden of the Hesperides, which provided the golden apples of immortality. The tree of good and evil, and the apple that Eve gave to Adam, in Genesis, is another of the stories that we can associate with Venus. When they both ate the apple, they became aware of their sexuality and were expelled from paradise, losing that inner place where they were at one with divinity. In Chinese culture, apples are a symbol of peace and apple blossoms are a symbol of feminine beauty.

VENUS AND THE ANCIENT GODDESSES

To understand the essence of the universal feminine force, we have to go back to the Palaeolithic and Neolithic periods of Old Europe. These peoples worshipped the great goddess, a total divinity reflecting the existence of a primal, life-giving energy, full of immense creative and transformative power. This deity includes both the "great mother", a symbol of fertility, and various goddesses who embodied other facets of feminine energy. The great goddess represented archetypal femininity: mysterious and powerful, the origin of all life with instinctual powers and supreme wisdom.

She represented mother nature and the power to generate life. She ruled over the elements and was creative and protective. However, she was also destructive and devouring, symbolizing all the cycles of life. She is the origin of the many archetypal goddesses that we can associate with both Venus and the Moon.

The ancient deities, heirs of the great goddess and associated with Venus, glorified love and physical pleasure. They enjoyed life, their bodies and their sexuality without seeking to please or expecting love in return. They exercised their immense power, actively expressed their desires, manifested their anger and shed blood. A characteristic of these goddesses was virginity, understood as integrity, since they had lovers, but were not defined by them.

In the cradle of civilization, goddesses such as Ishtar (Babylon), known as Inanna in Sumer, were associated with Venus. Inanna was a very powerful goddess, symbolizing feminine energy, life, nature, sexuality and beauty. She represented both love and war. As the supreme goddess, she ruled over heaven, Earth and the underworld. She was considered "the first-born of the Moon" and "the morning and evening star". She was a beautiful, sensual and flirtatious woman, but she could also be capricious and suffer fits of rage, which made this deity of love a terrible warrior. Many myths about Inanna, such as her descent to the underworld and subsequent return to the heavens, correspond to the movements of Venus across the celestial vault, which seemingly descends in the West and ascends again in the East. The goddess is able to confront her shadow, the most painful thing, and emerge triumphant. She returned victorious as a morning star to renew life and all that surrounded her. Inanna wasn't a passive or complacent goddess, characteristics now attributed to Venus; she was a reflection of the power of nature, which always breaks through and renews itself, making life possible. Knowledge of these goddesses makes it possible to understand Venus as a creative and powerful force beyond the sensuality, capacity for seduction and power of attraction traditionally attributed to her by the ancient Greeks. Other goddesses associated with Venus are Astarte (in Phoenician culture), Hathor (in Egypt), Lakshmi (in India), Freyja (in Norse mythology) and, of course, Aphrodite, the ancient Greek goddess of love and beauty.

VENUS AND ASTROLOGY

The Venus symbol

The astrological sign for Venus ♀ is also the symbol for femininity and women. It's known as the Venus symbol, and comprises a circle and a cross, similar to a handheld mirror. According to Greek mythology, the goddess always ensured that one of her servants held a mirror in front of her so that she could gaze upon her own beauty.

Aphrodite was the most beautiful of all the goddesses and possessed an irresistible charm. She was so beautiful that gods and mortals would fall at her feet. She was well aware of the effect she had, and it pleased her. This myth recounts how, in life, the vibrations we emit are reflected back to us in the most amazing of ways. Your life circumstances and your relationships are a perfect reflection of your inner self. Also, the people you attract in love are sometimes much-needed mirrors that show you where you are in your evolution. When you see yourself in that person, you always discover something important about yourself. You unconsciously project onto your relationships those aspects of your nature that you consider negative and find difficult to accept, in other words, the things that bother you about them are unacknowledged parts of you. On the other hand, you also project positive traits that you don't see in yourself, which you find fascinating when you see them in the other person. What makes you fall in love with them is also a reflection of you.

Relationships help us to heal. Many of the emotions that you experience as a couple alert you to the fact that there's something you're not paying attention to. If the behaviour of the person in front of you bothers you deeply or hurts you, it's worth investigating exactly what it is you're feeling. Often, certain words or attitudes from our partners, which may be totally innocent, arouse intense emotions that stem from deep unhealed wounds from a previous relationship, or even from your childhood. This causes us to react and hold that person responsible. Venus tells us that the source of negative feelings towards others is in our hearts and that it's our duty to take responsibility for our thoughts and emotions. When you get angry, you're actually angry with yourself; when you want to save the other person, you're actually trying to save yourself. Everything starts and ends in you. It's this projection that reveals the image you're generating. By understanding that everything is within you, you have the option to take charge of your emotional states and establish relationships based on energetic and romantic harmony, rather than on feelings of need, guilt or weakness. Most of the time, we don't see life how it truly is; we see it as we are. The good news is that the more connected you are with love, your own heart and your deep, authentic self, the less you'll be guided by these feelings. You will have a clearer perception of life and everything around you. This is why it's so important to work on your self-awareness and personal development – and astrology is a wonderful tool for this.

On the other hand, the way others treat you is merely a reflection of how you treat yourself and what you think of yourself, even if it is done unconsciously. Another person's behaviour towards you is evidence of your own inner attitude and what you're projecting. For example, if you're convinced that you're worthless, your relationships will magically reflect that attitude, becoming a source of dissatisfaction. Your partner will treat you as if you're worthless, as if you're easily replaceable.

Accepting yourself means being honest with yourself, being brave enough to look in a mirror and see all your imperfections and love them unconditionally. When you look in the mirror, what do you see? Do you see the real you or what you've been conditioned to believe is you? There are steps you need to take to learn to like yourself and feel comfortable in your own skin. To charm and captivate another person, you first have to fall in love with yourself. You attract what you put out there – it's no mystery.

Inner beauty

True beauty is found within, no matter how you look. Our shining goddess knows that the most beautiful things don't need to draw attention to themselves and encourages you to find value in something deeper than a physique or image. Your self-worth must be solid and unchanging, and beyond the opinion and judgement of others. We live in a world that's designed to rob us of our power and disconnect us from what's essential, selling us a false idea of happiness. We're told that we are our bank balance, our weight, our image or our number of followers on social media. Our self-esteem oscillates according to what we get from the outside. But if you look closely at nature, a flower doesn't need to compare its beauty with another flower to feel good. A tree grows majestically and needs no external validation – it doesn't have to look at the tree next to it to see if it's taller, more beautiful or leafier than it is. How many people have you met whose appearance is nothing like the stereotypical beauty standard, but yet they still have a charm and charisma that makes them uniquely attractive? This mystery is due to the fact that they feel that way, and the confidence they exude ends up captivating us. How many times have you fallen in love with someone who wasn't exactly a Greek god, and yet you still found them irresistible? Beauty doesn't respond to patterns, moulds or fashions, nor does it have anything to do with the external or the physical. It's a quality that emanates from the deepest depths of our soul; it's sensitivity, intelligence and confidence. There's nothing more beautiful than authenticity and expressing who we truly are. We all possess something uniquely beautiful. When you really tune into Venus' energy, you open up like a flower and express your natural and genuine beauty without fear, without comparing yourself to anyone else and without being conditioned by any ideals imposed by any society. If you connect with your astrological Venus goddess and express the ideal of the sign in which she's placed, your confidence will improve, and feelings of being attractive and feminine will be reinforced. Regardless of what you look like physically, the planet's energy can be cultivated and radiated and, believe me, feeling and strengthening Venus' energy is a perfect pre-date activity!

Venus' treasure

The things we love are a reflection of our soul. Our shining goddess invites you to connect with what you truly love and what truly gives you positive energy. She also encourages you to question how you can give yourself what you need to feel alive, full and satisfied. It's a matter of finding what you enjoy and what makes your heart feel full. It's about discovering the things that bring you so much joy that you could be immersed in them forever without distraction. The things you could do over and over again without ever getting tired, not because they're for financial gain, but because they make you feel radiant and full of energy.

With the wisdom of Venus we sow the vision of our heart. The planet is never too far from the Sun, never more than forty-eight degrees away. In my opinion, this is no coincidence. It indicates a great truth that we've forgotten: there's an intrinsic relationship between what we love and fully enjoy and our life purpose. The Sun is the centre of our inner universe and symbolizes how we consciously direct our will. The Sun illuminates us, gives us life and brings us joy. Indeed, the purpose of this experience we call life is to discover and express who we really are and to share that authenticity with the world. The positive energy you emanate when you allow yourself to be authentically you is truly powerful. When you're doing what you truly love and are passionate about, circumstances align to make it all possible. You're inherently abundant, rich and prosperous in the endeavours that align with your soul. When you tune into these powerful emotions, your potential to shape your reality is increased, and you easily attract what you deeply long for.

The position of Venus in your sign and house provides wonderful clues as to what we love and value internally, and can also reveal our inherent gifts. Within you, there are unique resources and abilities that are just waiting to be tapped into. If your Venus is in Sagittarius or in the 9th house, you will most likely love going on exciting adventures and travelling to faraway places to learn about other cultures and experience different ways of life. The goddess tells you that if you find the things you deeply love to do, you'll no longer need anyone to bring you that sense of fulfilment externally. You'll feel valuable, you'll know that you have something beautiful to offer, you'll develop your unique talents and your passion will give rise to endless creativity.

Venus wonderfully symbolizes self-love and how to find self-worth within ourselves, without needing to search for it externally. Never forget that believing in yourself deeply and loving yourself is a form of magic; if you can achieve this, you can make all your dreams come true. When you feel the power of a healthy self-evaluation, you begin to notice how the things that once attracted you change, suddenly becoming less interesting, and you realize that they no longer add anything to your life. You'll no longer need to cling to the first unknown person who crosses your path. Nor will you need someone else to "value" you or make you happy. You'll have the power to effortlessly provide yourself with this happiness and you'll stop needing to depend on someone else to fill any internal emptiness. You'll instinctively know when you need to let things go and when you need to let them flourish, when to give and when to receive, when to step away and when to stay. Essentially, you'll find the internal wisdom and balance necessary to be happy. You'll become the ruler of your own world and every day will feel magical – such is the power and the immense gift that this planet offers you.

This gift hides a surprise: once you feel passionate about what you do and are in tune with your heart's energy, you'll radiate a natural charisma that will be completely irresistible to others. Because you love yourself and feel complete, you'll know how to choose the right partner, the one who will bring something positive to your life and you to theirs, the one you want to share your happiness with.

Your relationship with yourself

The relationship you establish with yourself is the most essential, critical and lasting relationship you'll ever have. The quality of this relationship determines the quality of the relationships you forge with others, and by extension, with all of life. Imagine for a moment that instead of devoting all your effort and attention to making a relationship with that special person work, you invest all that energy into making the relationship with yourself infinitely stronger. Most of the time we ignore ourselves and go about our day on autopilot, unaware of how we feel and what our real needs are.

The shining goddess constantly reminds us that the way we feel isn't the result of what happens in our lives, but of how we interpret the circumstances. Our inner dialogue affects and determines our existence: how do you talk to yourself? Do you constantly point out your faults? Do you focus on your insecurities and the things you lack? Do you overlook the things you do well? Do you congratulate yourself on your achievements? When was the last time you let yourself know how amazing you are?

Make space in your life for yourself, and set aside quality time for yourself. Get away from everything that's bad for you. Take care of yourself first; give to yourself so that you can give to others. Do things that you enjoy and indulge yourself. If you're not satisfied, you'll have nothing to give. This isn't selfishness. Self-love is a starting point for growth.

Enjoy life

Throughout your experience in this reality, you'll attract various adventures and learnings, but that's not *all* life is about. You are here to experience happiness and joy. The energy of Venus connects us physically to life: we can enjoy it using our five senses. We perceive its essence when we look at a sublime sunset, a beautiful flower or a stunning landscape. It comes to us through music that touches our hearts and fills us with positive energy; through gorgeous paintings; through poems, words or stories that inspire and move us. Everything Venus casts its light on becomes magical, so it's no wonder that Venus features prominently in many artists' birth charts. Everything we find fascinating and that catches our attention has the planet's unmistakable mark. The planet invites us to discover the beauty of the world and to clearly perceive those sweet moments that remind us how wonderful it is to be alive. The shining goddess enhances our ability to see the beauty in everything, everywhere – in every one of our experiences, even the most unpleasant ones. Creativity and inspiration always appear in the here and now, when we're connected and enjoying ourselves, when we're taking a breath and being grateful for all the blessings we already possess, however small they may be. That's why our alchemical Aphrodite is related to any creative process.

Venus has an important connection with money and the simple pleasures of material life such as buying a nice dress, decorating your home, giving yourself a massage, eating at a good restaurant and pampering and indulging yourself in general. If hard aspects appear in your birth chart, you may feel a lack of self-esteem and experience a certain difficulty in enjoying life and connecting with pleasure. It can also cause problems in attracting what you desire and materializing and generating resources. On page 73 I explain briefly what the birth chart is all about and how you can use this book on a practical level.

Venus signs: Libra and Taurus

Venus is the ruling planet of two signs: Libra and Taurus. A ruling planet rules over a sign and a house because they have related energy. Venus in Libra and Taurus is a domicile Venus, and the planet feels especially comfortable because it can express its archetypal nature clearly. On page 75, you'll find a table containing the regencies. In the case of Venus, being ruler of Libra and Taurus, it has shades of both energies. In Taurus, Venus is receptivity and pure contemplation of life. It lives in the present and is open to receive what the world has to offer. It's easy-going yet difficult to move. It's comfort-loving, though it can be overly passive and indulgent. In Libra, Venus becomes more active and seeks encounters with others. It's related to love and the desire to find what complements us.

As the ruling planet of Libra, the planet symbolizes the things we like and the things we're attracted to. We choose one person over another because we love them and feel we're compatible. Through life's experiences we define our preferences, and they flow from us at all times. A Venus working helps us know how to recognize and discard what isn't good for us wisely. The goddess emphasizes the beautiful things in life and encourages living in harmony with everything around us. She symbolizes beauty and artistic expression in all areas: fashion, design, music, writing, painting... Aesthetic sensitivity, elegance and good taste are all touched by her magic wand. The moment we connect with our Venusian potential, our relationships acquire meaning and depth, and our creative life flourishes. This isn't just limited to the romantic and sexual, it's also about deep friendship, empathetic understanding, listening and sharing. It symbolizes your personal charm, which makes other people like you and feel attracted to your presence.

Taurus represents the yin side of Venus, where energy travels inwards to connect us with our physical body and its needs. It symbolizes the joy of being alive and enjoying experiences through the senses. The female body reflects nature and the Earth's energy. It's our ally. We must honour and respect it as sacred because it can lead us to fulfilment. To feel good, we need to listen to what it tells us and nourish it with the right foods. To love your body is to invest in pleasures that bring happiness and well-being and avoid everything that detracts from our health and energy. Moreover, with the daily choices we make from this space of love – such as choosing organic food, non-toxic cosmetics or preparing healthy meals – we're contributing to higher-quality, more sustainable consumption, which will help us move towards a world that is increasingly fair and more balanced, both with ourselves and with nature.

Men and Venus

We already know that Venus is the principle of attraction, the energy you emit that attracts a similar energy. It rules over your tastes and reflects the characteristics of the object of your desire – the thing that attracts your attention because you consider it aesthetically beautiful. Evidently, men also have Venus in their astrological charts. They have social skills, they exude charm and they're seductive. In modern society, more and more men take care of their appearance; they go to the gym, practise skincare, do their hair and buy nice clothes. However, there's always a part of the feminine essence that's harder to tap into. They naturally express their Mars, the archetypal warrior, and the ability to fight, compete and conquer – unless they're artists. This more refined feminine side is present in the male psyche, constituting the anima. In Carl Gustav Jung's analytical psychology, the anima refers to "the archetypal image of the eternal feminine" in the masculine unconscious, in other words it alludes to qualities men don't easily identify with and usually "project" onto a woman who embodies that feminine ideal, and thus becomes the object of their desire.

The woman that embodies the characteristics of their natal Venus by sign and by aspect will be the idealized living representation of beauty and men will feel hopelessly drawn to her or, at the very least, she will arouse their interest and they will find her unusually attractive. When a man looks at her, he will feel the urge to conquer her and experience romance. She's the female who will form the basis of all his erotic fantasies.

VENUS AND LOVE

Let there be spaces in your togetherness,
and let the winds of the heavens dance between you.
Love one another but make not a bond of love...
Fill each other's cup but drink not from one cup...
Sing and dance together and be joyous,
but let each one of you be alone,
Even as the strings of a lute are alone,
though they quiver with the same music.
KAHLIL GIBRAN

Venus symbolizes the desire to find a partner. You experience its beautiful transformation when you're attracted to another person and fall in love. The magical feeling of togetherness, of everything being right, or everything being perfect, is purely Venus. When you fall in love and it's reciprocated, you feel beautiful, unique and especially powerful, just like a goddess. You feel a joy that's hard to explain and life seems to flow unhindered. You enjoy every second of their company and wouldn't want to be anywhere else. One day you find yourself alone, and they flash across your mind, making you break out into a silly smile that lasts all day long. When you're at work, you can't help but remember the moments you've spent with them. At some point, you may even feel that feeling in your stomach, and then you realize there's no turning back; you're crazy about this person. Love transforms us and enriches our lives. It's a wonderful process. Suddenly we feel that we can take on the world and we dare to do things we never imagined we could do. Our perception of things changes; in fact, meeting that special someone changes everything. Is it magic? No, it's the alchemical effect of the goddess.

Venus' energy is feminine and receptive, she attracts what she desires, and because of this, she exudes magnetism and seductive power. The goddess fascinates and seduces the object of her desire by being authentic, and she doesn't have to do anything special to be liked. She is pure feminine energy, a heart that can open itself completely to the other person with no conditions. She doesn't offer affection, care or attention. She doesn't do anything concrete to be loved, and she doesn't depend on anyone to make her feel worthwhile. Radiating the planet means feeling confident in your beauty and attractiveness, and in winning over the person you like.

Venus rules the enjoyment of love, sexuality, sensuality and eroticism. She influences how you open yourself to a new love experience and how you give yourself to another. The goddess runs between lovers, giving them that magical feeling of perfection and fulfilment. She symbolizes that special chemistry which surrounds two people who are attracted to each other and want to be together. A cocktail of wonderful sensations is created in that "special bubble" that surrounds lovers and seems to insulate them from the outside world. When we experience this powerful attraction, we connect with the present and our senses are more awake than ever. The sensory experience is enhanced, the details of the other person's face are sharper, and their smell and touch produce a pleasurable sensation that's hard to forget… everything we experience is more intense, and we can feel our own heart beating.

Why don't you attract love?

To some extent, we all want to experience these incredible sensations and find that person who understands us without our having to utter a word; however, an intense desire for this isn't enough to conjure it up. There are times when our love life feels more like the Sahara Desert than an oasis brimming with life. You've made your request to the universe; you've performed all the love rituals you could find; you've written a long list of characteristics you want from your soulmate; you've harnessed the energy of the new moon to project your desire with intention, and you've even confidently and completely surrendered to the idea that it will all happen soon. The result? Nothing. You've done your part, but the universe seems to have taken a long holiday.

Venus' energy can often be inhibited, especially if there are hard aspects with Saturn. If that's the case, you'll have to make a special effort to get your inner Aphrodite to meet your needs, as this is an important way to feel good about yourself and open yourself up to love without anything standing in the way. We'll talk about this later, but for now let's look at other possible causes that are stopping you from attracting the person you desire.

Your unwilling unconscious

One of the reasons why you're not attracting a satisfying romantic relationship to your life may be that you're sending mixed signals – that's the mystery. Energy never lies; you're sending a very confusing message to the other person, to the universe and to yourself. You can consciously want a stable relationship, but on an unconscious level you may have a deep fear of commitment, or there may even be a part of you that loves to feel free and live with no strings attached, but you don't even know it yourself. Maybe you don't think you're worthy of love or worthy of being with an incredible person. Consequently, you behave in a way that doesn't align with what you want, or you choose a person who is nothing like what you really need. You want a relationship with the person of your dreams, but then you get into a romantic affair with someone who periodically ignores you and ends up driving you crazy. So you stand there, stalking their social media and waiting for a message that never comes when you expect it, but when the other person feels like it. Then the universe says "Aha! This is what you really want!" and keeps sending you this little gift. Exploring your astrological Venus with all its different aspects will help you illuminate those deep inner contradictions so that you can attract the relationship you want and give off energy with integrity instead of confusion. The parts of you that you don't recognize are more powerful than you can imagine. Be clear about the partner you want and wake up every morning with that idea in mind, and then don't accept anything that isn't aligned with that objective. The universe will test you and send you a person similar to the one before, but this time don't forget to say "no".

There are powerful mechanisms in our unconscious that are constantly creating our reality. The thoughts, actions and recurring beliefs you have about love can constantly sabotage your love life without you even realizing it. In fact, some beliefs are deeply implanted into our subconscious mind. For example, if you have experienced a bad relationship, or someone hurt you, or even if you have several failed romances behind you, you probably decided at some point that love isn't worth it, or that men just behave in a particular way. Somehow, these powerful convictions have settled inside you and may be blocking you from having a good relationship in the future. The psyche needs certainty, it wants security, and if you have only lived through experiences that have hurt you, how can you believe that there's hope for anything else?

One way to see if you have established negative beliefs is to observe how you talk about love, and what beliefs you hold about relationships when you're not directly thinking about the subject. For example, you're in a coffee shop talking to a friend who tells you about a bad experience with a man. You immediately identify with her, saying "Men are just..." In moments like these, saying such things can be trivial – but if you often find yourself saying things like this, then it may be worth investigating this resentment, because it's probably concealing a hidden belief. If this is the case, immediately replace it with another belief that's more favourable to you. Remember that you're in control of your next thought and can turn it into the new belief you'd prefer to have. You can even influence your next emotion and how you feel about love. Changing your perspective is a powerful tool that can transform everything in a matter of seconds.

Your last thought at night is the most important one of all, because it's incredibly powerful. You wake up in the morning on autopilot, which picks up from where you left off before you went to sleep, meaning that your first thought is connected to the last. As a result, your attitude during the day is similar to the one from the day before. I learned this during a "dream yoga" retreat years ago. Just before going to sleep, when you're so relaxed that you're about to drop off, you have an incredible opportunity to let your last thought influence your new life. We're constantly creating while we sleep, so make sure those last thoughts are geared towards manifesting your dreams.

Another powerful resource is positive affirmation. This refers to declarations that we express with power and conviction. We know that words have energy and what we say can either influence our lives positively or negatively; it's up to us. If we use these verbalizations correctly, we can change our state of mind almost instantly, bringing us into the perfect balance to manifest all the things we desire. What's more, if we say these phrases as if they were true, we trick our subconscious into recording these ideas without considering whether they're real or not, reprogramming our mind to externalize love. As a result, you become a magnet that attracts situations and circumstances that reflect what you believe. Make sure your sentences are short and clear, because this ensures that your subconscious doesn't get lost when following them.

Here are some examples:

- ★ "I am real, beautifully imperfect, uniquely beautiful and truly magic."
- ★ "I am a beautiful person who's worthy of love."
- ★ "I reclaim my feminine power now."
- ★ "My heart is open, and I give up all resistance."
- ★ "Romantic love is a wonderful experience."
- ★ "My relationships are healthy and stimulating."
- ★ "I love myself unconditionally."
- ★ "I love being a woman."

You're desperately searching for a relationship

Another reason you might not be manifesting a satisfying relationship is that you're unable to feel happy with your life and enjoy it until you have the relationship you so deeply wish and hope for. Don't put off having fun and adventures until you find a partner. Often, stepping forward and doing what your heart desires will lead you to love. Do whatever it is you feel like doing: learn something new or go on a special trip. Don't put it off until tomorrow; life is too short.

We've been conditioned since we were young girls to think that having a partner is one of the goals we need to obtain in order to achieve happiness. If we look at the films that we've been bombarded with ever since we were young, they all suggest that finding love is the most we can aspire to. Happy-ever-afters have caused a lot of damage. Many people only value and love themselves when they're in a relationship and if they're not, they drag around an uncomfortable feeling of inferiority. It's happened to all of us at some point during a romantic dry spell: we look at a happy couple as if they're living out their sweetest dream, while we're not. We all have that family member we see on special occasions who asks, "how's the love life?" In response, you put your game face on and catch yourself justifying your situation as if there's something you're not doing right. You can be made to feel like a bitter spinster if you're not in a relationship, especially if you're of a certain age. You can even hear people's thoughts in your head: "That girl must be weird, something must be wrong with her." But the truth is, there's nothing better than spending a long time alone to find yourself, enjoy life and discover all the things that make you feel alive. If you don't feel worthwhile, there's not much another person can do to give you what you lack. There's nothing sexier or more attractive than feeling good in your own skin and respecting yourself fully. There's nothing more seductive than knowing how to enjoy your life to the fullest by yourself and having interests that truly fulfil you. The most wonderful person in the world might come along, but if you don't value yourself, you won't be open to meeting them because you won't feel worthy of something so perfect.

In any area of life, when you want something, and you really go for it, you'll end up getting it. If you know what you want, focus on it, put all your energy into it and take action, eventually you get results. But believe me, the rules of love are different...

When you stubbornly pursue a relationship, all you do is block that relationship from appearing. No matter how much time you spend on the search, no matter how many times you swipe through dating apps or visit trendy places to look for that perfect person, you'll get nowhere. If you're desperate to find a partner, you're likely to give off impatient energy at the beginning of the relationship, which will make your potential partners run away in terror at the first opportunity. If you open yourself to love out of neediness, you'll only attract people who don't feel good either. Instead of improving your life, this will more than likely bring you more problems. You may even cling to "any partner" to avoid being alone, which will cause you to experience disappointment and disillusion over and over again...

One day, you get tired of waiting and decide to focus on yourself and start to enjoy your own company. Your energy transforms, making you feel good. Without realizing it, you forget to look for that perfect person. You no longer consider being alone an issue; on the contrary, you've been without a partner for a long time, but you don't really care – you've accepted it. One day you go out with your friends without any intention of meeting anyone, and what happens? You suddenly meet this person. The relationship you wanted appears out of nowhere, just when you thought it was impossible, just when you didn't care... It's funny, isn't it?

You don't make space

You've got a busy life, full of plans, routines and work. You don't have time for a relationship. It's not that you don't want one, but you're always working, and when you do have free time, you veg out to watch TV or you go to the same old places with the same people because it's more comfortable that way. You're unconsciously closing yourself off from love, perhaps out of fear, or perhaps because you prefer to do life alone, which is to be respected. But if you truly desire a relationship, you'll have to make space for it in your life and start setting aside more free time. When we meet someone new, we have to dedicate time to them. If you don't have any spare time to offer, then that perfect person won't have a chance to appear. You'll also need to switch up your life: go to new places, make different plans, break free from dreary routines. Let your hair down and do something completely different.

Another way you might not be making space is by remaining infatuated with a previous relationship. Perhaps you haven't forgotten about that person and long to see them again, even if you know it's impossible. Or maybe you're in an on–off relationship with someone who keeps appearing and disappearing, keeping you stuck and not letting you move on. You can't wallow in your suffering or hold on to vain hopes. Remember that it's not what you lack that hurts you, but the belief that you need it. You must move on and let go of what no longer brings you any joy or fulfilment. You must open up to new things with confidence.

To manifest the relationship you desire, you need to close previous relationship cycles. You might say, "It's been ages since I've been with anybody", or "My ex has been history for months", and that might be true on a conscious level. You might think that a chapter of your life is over, and *physically* that might be true, but *energetically* it might not be. Energetic ties are invisible strings that bind us to people from our past with whom we had an intense relationship. These relationships don't necessarily have to be long-lasting; they just need to have left a powerful mark. During the relationship, these people may have been positive and necessary, but if we're not able to cut them off at the end of the relationship, they become limiting and harmful ties that can extend that chapter of your life, even if you're no longer with that person. Proof of this is recurring dreams about them. If you feel that there are still invisible ties that bind you to a previous relationship, you need to let it go with the power of your intention. The antidote is to spend some time alone in deep healing. There are very effective meditations that help you let go of past relationships. They work directly with our second energy centre, located in the womb area. This is where we accumulate the sexual energy of our partners. The best thing to do is to use the energy of the black moon, two days before the new moon, which is an ideal energetic and emotional moment for introspection since we're more perceptive and intuitive at this time. This window of time is the most powerful in terms of cleansing, purifying and letting go of everything that is energetically useless. Meditate, feel this space and record the emotions you feel or the images that come to mind, and let them flow. Remember that you are your own best oracle; no one knows you better than you. Find that moment to listen to yourself, go within and connect with your inner wisdom.

You don't want to open your heart

Often we go through life wanting to find someone that we have a deep connection and real intimacy with, but when they appear, we're unable to open ourselves up to this relationship without feeling fearful. We don't want to suffer or openly show our vulnerabilities, because we're afraid of things going wrong again. Everyone has had their heart broken, not just once, but multiple times. We've all felt pain, but this mustn't make you close up completely. It's often the case that certain types of relationships leave us with some trauma, and when we meet a new person and start to feel something for them, or when things start to get "serious", we unconsciously pull away or sabotage the relationship. Personal relationships will always require us to take risks, because we have to put our trust in the other person. It's through our connection to another that we discover ourselves and reach our full potential. Through relationships, we grow and become more conscious. The romantic relationships that we experience, especially those that touch us deeply, represent an opportunity for enormous transformation since they teach us a lot and force us to learn from our mistakes. Through love, we feel one of life's most intense pains. Just like in the myth of Inanna, we venture down into the underworld and confront our demons, only to emerge fully renewed, much wiser and strengthened by the experience.

Feminine sexuality

The goddess is present in every sexual encounter. Her highest essence corresponds to a conscious, unconditioned sexual openness. She symbolizes the exchange of energy that takes place on several levels during a sexual relationship, which helps us improve our connection and intimacy with the person we love. A healthy connection is joyful, pleasurable, erotic, sensual, free, blissful, passionate, deep, loving and intimate. When we integrate all the planet's potential, we improve our relationship with our body and our sexual cycles, and we re-establish our capacity to connect with fun, joy and pleasure.

Numerous ancient cultures saw something sacred in every expression of life on Earth. They believed that every living being, as well as the planet itself, was an expression of the divinity that dwells within. We're all connected to the flow of life and all have value thanks to the mere fact that we are alive. These peoples saw the scared in everything around them, even in the most mundane, and sexuality was part of this elevated worldview. For these peoples, sexual energy was a very powerful part of the flow of life and was considered sacred. In numerous texts we find that the act of sex was a form of alchemy. The union between two beings wasn't a mere reproductive act, nor a way to obtain instant gratification, but rather a way to elevate the conscience and feel divinity on Earth. The vagina was revered and considered both the gateway to this world and the doorway back to the infinite. Sexuality was the means for men and women to reach transcendence, achieve success and connect with the energy of the goddess. This was the alchemical power of Venus: the deep and joyful encounter between two bodies, which leads to a transformation that has the potential to regenerate health and vitality, increase our positive energy and put us in balance with the universe.

With time, these beliefs and traditions were lost due to the rise of monotheistic religions. The body started to be seen as impure and separate from the spirit. The repression of women and female sexuality, as well as the exploitation of nature, began to occur simultaneously as other ways of understanding life developed. For centuries, our sexuality has been rejected, and this part of our essence relegated purely to procreation. The expression of Venus was emasculated, covered with stigmas and darkness. We're still unconsciously burdened with guilt stemming from the concepts of sin and punishment. We were taught that a woman shouldn't express exuberance, eroticism or provoke desire in another. This rejection has produced many barricades to expressing our full potential as women. However, the sacred power of Venus emerges when we refuse to be limited by social conditioning or conventional family obligations, when we belong to no one but ourselves. Our shining goddess is the essence of true female empowerment, which is why she's been so feared and persecuted.

Although we've liberated ourselves sexually, we still fail to understand the true potential of the planet, and its archetype is one of the least integrated in our society today. The male model of sexuality, in which sex seems like a race to reach a goal rather than a journey in which we can find joy and connection, has even been imposed on the female. The consequence is that, for many women, reaching orgasm becomes an agonizing pressure that prevents them from fully enjoying the experience. If they don't "deliver" what is expected of them, if they don't reach the goal, they can be burdened with deep dissatisfaction. Sexual expression in women is much more complex, rich and broad than it is in men, who are generally much more direct, impulsive and primal and, in principle, don't need an emotional connection to feel satisfied. Our sexual energy blossoms more effortlessly when we feel loved and valued. This results in greater relaxation, which helps us to enjoy the act more and experience greater satisfaction. Feminine sexuality involves giving and receiving, and we are attuned to the Moon, Venus and Mars in unison. In fact, we have one organ whose sole function is to generate sexual pleasure: the clitoris.

Sex is a completely sensory experience involving the whole body. Unfortunately, sexuality is linked to body image and self-esteem. It seems that we can only openly enjoy sexual intercourse if we have a certain physical appearance or if we're the perfect weight. Sometimes what we desire in sex, what instinctively roars within us, can be far removed from what's culturally accepted or considered normal for a woman. Satisfying our true instinctual nature reconnects us with our life force and our creative energy.

You need to align yourself with your Venusian energy if:

- ★ Asking for what you need and deeply desire from a sexual encounter overwhelms you.
- ★ You don't open yourself fully in a sexual relationship and find it hard to connect with your innermost self.
- ★ You often feel unsatisfied after sexual experiences.
- ★ You find it difficult to relax into the joy, pleasure and love that comes from a sexual connection.
- ★ You don't feel confident about your naked body, or you experience shame in front of the person you like.
- ★ You're not in touch with your body, your sensuality, the depths of your wildest nature or your natural rhythms.

We know that sexual energy is intensely powerful and creative, since it has the capacity to generate life. Because of this, it's vital that this energy isn't blocked and that it can flow freely. Fortunately, we're starting to become aware of this and feminine energy is undergoing a resurgence. This powerful energy is part of our second energy centre, located in the pelvis and stomach. This is our cauldron where we have the power to make magic.

Next, I'll put forward a meditation that will help you tune into this warm and restorative energy. It includes a visualization to help you understand your relationship with the energy of Venus and attune to it, and in this way, you can give life to the flower that lies dormant in your womb.

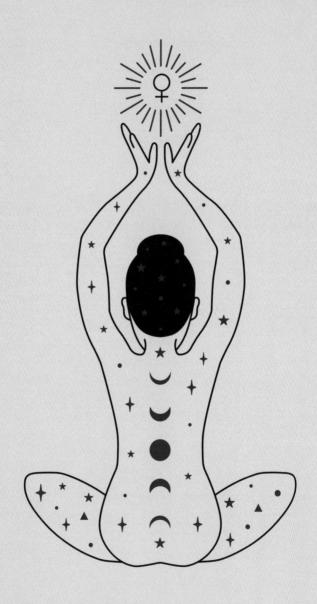

VENUS MEDITATION

1. Find a place where you can be alone and no one can interrupt you. Cleanse the space with incense, sage or palo santo. Dim the lights in your room; it'll be easier for you to move inwards if the place is in semi-darkness. Sit comfortably with your back straight, on a chair or cushion. Close your eyes and remain silent for a few seconds.

2. Next, visualize a golden-white light cascading from your head to the soles of your feet. Breathe deeply, bringing your attention to your belly area. Inhale and exhale. Feel how your breathing relaxes. To breathe is to feel at one with everything. Feel how each breath holds the opportunity to love and be loved. Feel how each breath opens space to manifest everything you desire in your life.

3. Think back to a time when you enjoyed life, when you felt very happy and joyful. Bring that powerful memory back to the present and recreate the feeling of well-being and fulfilment. Experience those emotions again and notice how you feel a warm smile on your face. Are you tuned in? Now bring that smile to every cell in your body and thank every part of you for its function. Love and smile at every part of your body: your face, your neck, your breasts... Stop when you feel it necessary. Take your time; there's no hurry.

4. Now, bring your attention to the soles of your feet and imagine that long roots are penetrating deep into the Earth. Smile at the feminine energy that dwells within them and feel it smile back at you. You might feel a tingling on the soles of your feet or a warm, subtle energy. May-

be you'll feel your smile widen. Don't worry if you don't feel anything, the only thing that matters is to relax, without trying to maintain control over anything.

5. Bring your attention inward, to the area around your uterus, in your pelvis. Send the feeling of well-being to that area, which is the centre of your feminine essence and creative power. Simply becoming aware of your uterus and feeling its energy is a real revelation and allows you to experience a state of peace.

6. Calmly, now that you're in this state of mind, visualize a flower. Take time to examine how it looks in your mind. Take in all the details, take in its scent. What does it look like? Is it open or closed? Is it beautiful? How do you feel when you look at it? What sensations do you feel when you look at it? What qualities could you attribute to it? Is it refined, exuberant, delicate...? What does it radiate? Does it reflect purity, beauty, eroticism...?

7. Put that flower in context – where is it located? Has it been easy to find? It may be a wild orchid deep in a jungle, a beautiful rose in a garden, a lotus flower in the middle of a pond or just another daisy in the countryside. It might stand alone on a cold valley floor, or on a mountaintop. It might be a pure flower in a crystal urn, or be in a temple that's difficult to reach. There are no limits to the imagination. What do you think it needs to bloom to the fullest? Apart from the flower, have any other images come to mind?

8. Imagine you're that flower, unfolding its beauty and fully opening all its petals without fear. Imagine that you live in the here and now, connected to what's around you and to your roots in the Earth that sustain you. The Sun is your nourishment, the air lightly sways you. You exhale a magical perfume. Your beauty and scent represent a strong attraction, even if you don't intend it. Imagine you're that flower that lives in harmony with everything around it, that doesn't have to struggle, that's blooming at exactly the right moment.

9. Open your eyes slowly; take your time. When you're ready, write down everything that emanates from inside of you on a piece of paper. Write down how you feel in detail. Write down what your flower is like, everything that you've experienced and felt. If you feel uncomfortable during the meditation, open your eyes and write down your feelings.

MARS AND VENUS: THE DANCE OF OPPOSITES

The entire universe is ruled by two forces in a constant state of attraction. In nature, there's always a force that emits and a force that receives. Taoism talks of yin and yang, Hinduism reflects this duality in the figures Shiva and Shakti, and Tantra also speaks of feminine and masculine energy. In the Zodiac, the twelve signs represent the totality of life's energy and the complete spectrum of the potential of human experience. The twelve signs are divided into six masculine and six feminine signs. This doesn't refer to what we would today understand as gender, but rather to their energy qualities. The masculine signs are Aries, Gemini, Leo, Libra, Sagittarius and Aquarius, and they're associated with extraversion, action, the spirit of conquest and activity. They do things outwardly, they're forward-looking and make their mark on the world. When they want something, they go for it rather than waiting for it to happen. The feminine signs are Taurus, Cancer, Virgo, Scorpio, Capricorn and Pisces, and are associated with introversion, receptivity, attraction, stability and are oriented to the past. They act in a subtle and reserved way, receiving a mark from the world. We all have both energies within us, regardless of our gender. The planets are in charge of attuning to the different vibrations of each sign and depending on them, we'll express certain qualities over others.

Mars and Venus symbolize the cosmic dance between the feminine and the masculine, the opposites that attract and complement each other. They represent another way of expressing the Sun and the Moon, that is, the masculine and the feminine in us. Mars is action, Venus is attraction and receptivity. Mars is the urge to exist as an individual separate from the environment, with personal desires and motivations. It represents the ability to use our will to achieve what we want. Both planets form the eternal balance between giving and receiving, between the "I" and the "you". With Mars, I make decisions, fight, assert myself and act in the world; with Venus I contemplate, receive, listen and please. One pole can't exist without the other. Both energies walk hand in hand; they need and attract each other. They're two sides of the same coin. Balancing both archetypes is no easy task, but it's essential to build healthy bonds. Emotional satisfaction in a relationship is achieved when we find ways to balance our need for freedom and independence with our need for intimacy and connection. Love is a complex experience, during which, time and again, we must resolve the eternal dilemma of how to be an individual while remaining emotionally attached to another human being. Having a solid relationship without losing ourselves and compromising our individuality is complicated, but achievable.

Women identify more with their feminine energy and seem to have been programmed to be patient and compassionate. We always mediate conflicts, even those counter to our own opinions, and we always prioritize connection over confrontation. The rejection of masculine energy affects women deeply, making them dependent. Many women desperately need compliments to be happy, and if they don't get them they carry around a sense of inner emptiness, as if something is missing. In many cases, they find themselves experiencing toxic and harmful relationships, but are unable to end them. If you feel this is the case for you, you must learn to reckon with your desires and respect yourself on a personal level. We must understand the different roles we play in a relationship in order to be able to transform them. Moreover, dynamic exchanges and healthy relationships are all about learning to give and receive on equal terms.

I imagine this as each individual within the relationship pulling one end of a rope. The rope always needs to maintain the right tension to keep the relationship good and stable. If both people pull at the same time, the rope becomes too taut and breaks. Conversely, if one of the two always pulls, while the other always gives in, the necessary tension is lost, and the relationship becomes unbalanced. Ideally, for the relationship to be equal, one partner should pull once, and the other should accompany that movement, and vice versa.

We always have one planet more boosted than another; no one is one hundred percent balanced. We're attuned to one type of energy according to our birth chart, and often it has nothing to do with our gender. For example, if a woman has a majority of planets in masculine signs or has these signs at important angles (such as the ascendant or midheaven), it will motivate her to act and go for what she wants. If you have Mars in a predominant position in your chart (in the 1st and 10th houses, for example), it will be easy for you to make decisions and assert yourself in the world. For your life to be in balance, you must be able to manifest the planets you have in masculine signs and show a receptive attitude to the planets you have in feminine signs. We can't act in a meaningful way if we don't perceive and evaluate the situation correctly first. Developing both archetypes separately and finding ways to use them in a balanced way is very important. If you reject the yang or masculine energy, you'll feel weak, anxious, oversensitive and tend to victimize yourself. You'll lack motivation, find it difficult to focus and feel like you're not in control of your life. You'll understand how important it is to use both energies to have a healthy relationship.

Facing away from Mars

There are various indicators that you're facing away from Mars in your relationships. Let's take a look at them.

You're too adaptable

You're always available when your partner wants to see you. Remember that you have your own life, your own friends and your own plans. Don't give up everything for that one person. You also have to fill your life with things that are yours alone. It's important for everyone to have their own space; you don't need to share everything. I'm convinced that if you maintain your independence, hobbies and interests, and do things outside the relationship that *you* find fulfilling, fun and happy, you'll be much more interesting to your partner by extension.

You have a passive attitude

When we start a relationship, everything is wonderful. We feel as if we're floating on cloud nine and want nothing more than simply to be with that person. When we're in love, we tend to praise our loved one's virtues and ignore their flaws. The less we know them, the more we project our unconscious desires onto them. The joy and happiness we feel blinds us, and we only see what we want to see. As we get to know them, the first disappointments begin to set in. Let's not fool ourselves, the other person is only human, and so are we. We know that the perfect relationship doesn't exist; there are moments when things flow effortlessly and there are others when friction arises. You may love everything about them, but the day will come when something happens that makes you feel bad; it may be something they've said, a funny comment that wasn't funny, a particular attitude, a strange behaviour... Then you notice that something has sparked inside of you, and you realize that feeling in your stomach is no longer butterflies. The best way to react in this moment is make your feelings known, gently but firmly. We often don't express these feelings because we want to preserve beautiful moments and not put a dampener on things. If there's one thing I've seen for myself, it's that when you don't express yourself honestly, it attracts an energy that stops the relationship from flowing as beautifully as it did before. It casts a sort of shadow over the relationship, planting a seed of separation. If we let these feelings accumulate, it will end in deep resentment. Without realizing it, we'll fall into destructive patterns that will continually threaten the relationship. If you notice the other person is trying to manipulate you, or they express an opinion that isn't correct, or you simply have a different opinion, say so! Don't try to please them to avoid a moment of tension. If you don't like one of their suggestions, let them know and suggest something else. If you always just agree with your partner, let them make all the decisions and force yourself to do things you don't feel like doing, you'll end up accumulating feelings of resentment and dissatisfaction, which will be very harmful for you and for the relationship in the long run. Don't say "yes" when you really mean "no". Always communicate what you feel, tell them your preferences and what's important to you. Communication and dialogue should be the basis of every relationship.

You don't know what you're looking for in love

Every time we begin a relationship, we should ask ourselves what we want and expect from it. Otherwise, we might find ourselves in a love story without knowing what we really want from that connection. We then project unclear, contradictory and complicated signals. Of course, this is a vicious cycle because if you don't know what you want, you can't express it either, and the other person will feel really lost. What do you want from love? What are you looking for in a relationship? What are your expectations? What are your needs? What do you really want? Is this relationship good for you? Does it support who you are in this moment of your life? It's crucial that you work on your self-awareness because you can only find out what you want by knowing who you are. Once you know what you want, you can make the right choices, both in love and in life.

You don't establish healthy boundaries

If you don't assert yourself when your partner does something to hurt you, you definitely need to work on your Mars. If your partner doesn't value you, doesn't take you into account, ignores you, belittles you and you allow them to do so, you must learn to bring out your fire and demand the respect you deserve. Don't make yourself small to make that person feel comfortable. Don't shrink for someone who refuses to grow up and doesn't want you to grow up either. Don't extinguish your own light so that the other person can shine. Listen to your inner voice and don't ignore your instincts; if you feel bad, you're tolerating things you don't want to. In any relationship, you have to be clear about your boundaries from the beginning. Connect with what you want and what you deserve, so you know what you're willing to accept and what you're not. When you don't, you're giving up your power, and you're teaching the other person how to treat you. I promise you that it's very difficult to redirect this situation later on. Always remember never to accept less than you deserve; don't get attached to anyone who doesn't give you the same love that you give them. A person who doesn't respect your time and considers you their last resort isn't worth it. If the person you like doesn't give you what you want, it's time to rethink your romance. If you're still in love, it will undoubtedly be one of the hardest things you'll ever have to do in your life, but it's crucial to stop being attached to someone who's not ready to love you. Let go. If you do, you'll open up space to find an authentic and genuine relationship that's more in tune with what you want.

You don't make decisions about the relationship

Often, we prolong emotional relationships that are stagnant and no longer nourish or vibrate with us. If you're in a relationship that no longer helps you grow or brings you joy and you don't make the decision to leave it behind, you're not aligned with your fire. Your desire is a gauge you can use to work out if something has run its course. If you look at your partner and feel indifferent and no longer sense the spark you used to feel, oh my friend, you're in trouble... If you never feel like doing anything they suggest and find yourself almost forcing yourself to do it, forcing something that doesn't flow over and over again, it's time to cut it off. Even if you've tried time and again to improve the connection, you must accept that you've hit a brick wall. Don't try to persist; the romance has run its course. Everything that no longer appeals to you signals the need for an end, or at least a profound change and reorientation. When it's no longer possible to reach agreements within the relationship that make you both feel happy and satisfied, it's time to let go of that connection and make room for a new relationship with a better chance of success. Remember that it's decisions and not circumstances that determine your life, and a timely withdrawal is always a victory. Life is short, don't waste your time.

You constantly need approval

Your endeavours are always conditioned by the approval of others. Unconsciously, you always look for validation externally. Every time you do something, you ask the people around you for their opinion and confirmation because you're not confident enough to bring your wishes to fruition on your own: "Do you like this? Is this okay?" If they say no, you might find yourself rethinking all your decisions. We all like to be supported by others; there's something very special about the feeling of warmth it creates in us, and that's not necessarily a bad thing. It works against us when everything we do or every decision we make has to be consulted. Sometimes doing what you really want means being at odds with your partner or the people around you. If you hold back from doing what you want because of what they might say or because you don't want to make anyone unhappy or overstep the mark, or because you think others won't like it and won't think it's right, you'll end up regretting it. Wanting to keep everyone happy, make everyone like you and make a good impression is commendable, but in time you'll discover that you can't please everyone.

You don't know how to be alone

You always need to be with someone; you don't know how to be happy without a partner. You leave one relationship and soon find yourself in another. Deep down, you're afraid of being alone. I know many women that have spent years in one relationship, leaving the other person to sort everything out. It's as if they don't know how to live without them and are reduced to the level of "little girls" who look to "daddy" to solve their problems. When the relationship ends, they're left devastated and feel totally incapable, and they find it takes a lot to restore their self-confidence. They can even feel as if they've lost their own identity. The antidote to this is to learn to be alone. Being single for a long time prepares you for a healthy relationship in the future, as it's a unique opportunity to focus on you. If you do things on your own, without relying on others, you'll feel great. You'll radiate an incredibly attractive strength and power. In addition, this approach to life ensures that you'll have high levels of autonomy, which results in romantic relationships free of dependency – a true gift.

Understanding our true desires

We've been deeply conditioned to believe that we should desire certain things: a partner, a big house, a nice car, children, money... We've been taught how to dress, how to love, what to study... We've not been taught to look inside ourselves and recognize what we truly want. We're an infinite consciousness capable of being and creating whatever we want, but we're programmed to perceive our limitations and not the power we have. Mars' energy represents an invitation to explore your personal desires, so you can become aware of why you're struggling with certain things, the reasons behind why you do the things you do and what's driving you. Desires are powerful processes, and even if they're unconscious, they guide your actions. Mars pushes you to pursue what you're passionate about and let go of the desires that are no longer aligned with who you are. But to achieve this, you must properly exercise the power of introspection and reflection.

How do you relate to yang or masculine energy? What is behind your desires, actions and impulses? Are they authentic and genuine desires, or are they conditioned? What emotions influence the important decisions in your life? Do you dare to forge your own path, or do you live conditioned by the validation of others? How do you assert yourself in the world? What fires your soul? What motivates and inspires you? What are you fighting for? What do you really want? Why do you want it? What are you willing to sacrifice for it? Will you be able to handle it once you get it?

These are some important questions you can ask yourself to try to find out to what extent you're aligned with your inner fire. Following the path that leads to realizing your desires and daring to live the experiences that will allow you to grow and develop will help you understand how to choose your partners better and how not to depend on them. When you have doubts about any circumstance in your life, turn inwards and find your true courage, the courage that comes from deep within you. When you tune into it, you'll feel assured that you're being guided and there's absolutely nothing to fear.

Expressing our anger

It was historically men who went out into the world to fight, to be warriors and conquer other lands. They were the pioneers, the adventurers and the entrepreneurs, and it was more common to find them in positions of power and wealth. Most women were limited to developing their Mars indirectly, defending their own in the sphere of home and family. We've certainly not had it easy, and the woman who dared to be independent and chart her own path defied society. Historically, the figure of a strong, combative woman hasn't been widely accepted. Instead, "strong women" were considered problematic, dangerous and not "fit" for marriage and motherhood. Showing strength and power was unbecoming in a woman. This has led to many women still having problems expressing their anger even today, as an angry woman is seen as "hysterical", "neurotic" or outright "deranged". A person in an abusive situation won't get out of it by smiling and using good manners, she'll get out of it by connecting with her rage and expressing her anger. We need positive aggression to awaken the strength within us and bring an end to the situations we want to change. Of course, anger shouldn't run rampant, but recognizing these instinctive emotions and channelling them positively is fundamental to finding balance. If we don't express certain emotions, they'll accumulate and become ticking time bombs that will explode when given the right stimulus. We'll carry feelings of restlessness, anxiety and discomfort with us. Moreover, if we bottle up these feelings without giving them an adequate outlet, they can become potentially destructive emotions and even create health problems, such as physical pain and depression (it's believed that one of the facets of this disorder is related to unexpressed anger).

If you only identify with your feminine energy and reject your warrior side, you'll project that pent-up energy outwards and attract things that can be made up of aggression: hurtful, domineering, imperative, bossy people who take advantage of you or talk down to you. Observe and reflect on what your relationships are like and what they're showing; if you don't recognize these emotions, you're likely to attract certain experiences so that you can become aware of the part of yourself that you're ignoring. Mars is the planet with which we assert ourselves; if you reject it for fear of its negative manifestation, you're denying yourself the opportunity to realize your potential and, as a consequence, you'll be lumbered with feelings of unworthiness, which will also affect your personal relationships.

Female empowerment?

When we focus too much on the masculine side and disconnect from our true essence, we become controlling, impulsive and dominant. Everything has to be as we say, it's our way or the highway. We constantly want things, and once we get them, we want more. We're never satisfied, we never have enough. We hunt down new goals and objectives, but we don't stop to enjoy what we've achieved. When we desire something intensely, we go for it, without considering the consequences of our actions nor the implications that this desire may have on the environment or on our own lives. We compete with each other because we feel that there isn't enough for all of us and that someone could take away what we've achieved. We're burdened with the feeling that we're not "enough". We feel that we have to give more and more and be the best at everything… How exhausting! If we isolate ourselves in the masculine, the result is a scarcity mentality. We become individualistic, lonely and self-centred, and detach ourselves from others. We become disconnected from our feminine bodies and live only in our minds, and we make all our decisions from there. We become so focused on the future that we overlook life and forget to enjoy the little things in the here and now.

Although we're slowly assuming our power, we often embody a distorted masculine role. This makes us feel increasingly confused about our true place in the world. Many women are increasingly taking on and occupying positions of responsibility and leadership. They need to employ these qualities in the world since, when it comes to goals, masculine energy needs to blossom to its fullest, and that's fine. However, we live in a very competitive society, and we've gone to the other extreme, losing our true power. We fight and we get things done, but because we don't act from the depths of our feminine energy, we end up feeling terribly empty. We think we're in control, but it's only an illusion. We're building houses out of a deck of cards, and any move we make could bring it all crashing down.

On the other hand, we've suffered so much throughout history that we've adopted an extremely defensive position towards the masculine. This generates a lot of conflict in modern relationships, to the point that some women choose to remain single because they feel that this is the only way they can fully develop. It would seem that if you pursue your dreams, you can't enjoy a deep, solid loving relationship. Traditionally, the figures of female fighters and warriors have been women who are independent, lonely and uninterested in romantic partners or commitment. We've inherited these old stigmas, and today we unconsciously feel that we must choose between being loved and accommodating any and all of our partner's whims, or being strong and alone. Have you ever feared getting involved in a new relationship because you stopped doing things that were important to you in order to adjust to your previous partners? Don't worry, you're not the only one who has. Fortunately, this is changing, but we still have a long way to go. Choosing solitude may be a valid option, but in my opinion, a relationship represents a huge opportunity for self-discovery.

Reclaiming our feminine power

In the modern world, we've become disconnected from our natural rhythms; we need to return to the feminine essence, which is where our true power lies. Feminine energy is life, healing, wisdom and love. Only from the feminine can we properly co-connect with the masculine. Venus will only prosper if Mars also prospers. Our world needs more feminine energy: more receptivity, gentleness, openness and slowness.

There are many things you can do to feel the feminine energy within you again, to reconnect with yourself, with your body and with your creative depth.

- ★ Connect with music that makes you vibrate, dance, sing and let go of control.
- ★ Go for a walk in a forest, calm your mind, feel nature, look at the moon, watch the stars, awaken your senses.
- ★ Enjoy a sunset or a sunrise. Go out and feel the sun, wind or rain on your skin. Find a way to connect with nature in a way that feels effortless and makes you feel good.
- ★ If possible, hug a big, old tree. Feel how its energy envelops you. Notice how the vibration of nature calms and heals you. Realign yourself with the flow of life and feel its heartbeat again.

★ Remind yourself that nothing needs to be done. There are no goals, there's only the here and now. There's nothing to prove, there's only being. Release the tension in your shoulders, let it all go, breathe in and breathe out.

★ Remember that you're always growing, changing and adapting; that's what makes you beautiful.

★ Feel at one with the universe. Feel completely confident in your life's path. You don't have to worry about anything, because everything you need is already available to you.

★ Breathe deeply and let the vibrations soothe you. Take a deep breath and let go of everything that no longer serves you. Release your fears with each exhale. Breathing is fundamental when it comes to connecting with your surroundings, helping you to make space in your mind and body and by extension, in your life. It releases muscle tension, anxiety and any blockages that you may have built up.

★ Feel gratitude in your heart every day, and the universe will begin to give you more beautiful things to be grateful for. It's a truly powerful experience to fully realize and acknowledge all the things you have to be grateful for. Don't forget to appreciate yourself too; be thankful for your virtues, your wisdom, your willingness to evolve and the work you do in this world. This will help you learn to love yourself in a different way.

★ Accept the present, don't reject it. Even if your situation is extreme or painful, make peace with it. There's no mistake – you're in the right place at the right time. Feminine energy is always ready to surrender, and from that place it conquers and overcomes any situation.

★ Surround yourself with other women. This will help you rebalance the feminine in you. After all, when we spend a lot of time with other women, even our periods synchronize.

★ Find that sacred space for yourself where you can reconnect with your dreams. Open the windows and remove any objects that make you feel stressed or stir up negative emotions.

★ Do something creative. Tune into your inspiration and align with your Venus... If you love to paint, paint. If you love to write, write. Do what you love, and if you can't remember what that is, think back to when you were a child. What did you like to do then?

As you connect with your feminine power, that invincible force in you, you'll let go of control and impatience and you'll start to feel your creativity flow. Everything has its moment. Things happen at just the right time – never too soon, never too late – so rushing them is useless. You have to trust in the process. For a seed to blossom into a flower, it needs time to mature. Tune in to your Venus and increase your vibration; abundance will naturally flow into your life. Nature is abundant, life is abundant. Abundance is feminine, it's feeling that there's more than enough for everyone and there's no need to fight or compete for resources.

Express what you feel in every moment; don't be afraid to be yourself. Be brave enough to show your vulnerability, be authentic, be weird, be free, be real, be wild. Be brave enough to be who you are, because you never know who might love that beautiful woman you try so hard to hide. You are and always have been enough.

The feminine connection with Mars

We all need to be free and develop that little bit of rebelliousness necessary to act as we please. This can be mistaken for selfishness from the outside, but it's the exact opposite. Mars' energy is that spontaneous and direct action that dares to step out of the comfort zone and into the unknown; it represents the will to move forward with determination and a fighting spirit. If you consciously harness the powerful energy of the red planet, you might happen upon the opportunity to let go of debilitating attitudes and beliefs, and become stronger and more resilient to adversity. The connection to Mars as a woman restores our ability to make clear choices about our life direction. Through its energy, we connect with the ferocity to protect what we love and defend our freedom. It makes us want to follow every impulse that arises within us without restriction or limitation. It represents integrity and an "I can take care of myself" attitude that makes it possible for us to pursue our own goals with courage and self-confidence. Claiming our fire is to connect with the desire to be what we have the capacity to be, to know what really makes us happy deep in our hearts and move in that direction.

THE VENUS SIGNS

Your birth chart is a symbolic representation of the cosmos at the time of your birth. It reflects your entire energetic structure. It's an exact and detailed map of your strengths and character traits: behaviour, way of thinking, desires, motivations, way of relating to others, emotions, challenges, talents, blocks, fears... It isn't how you perceive yourself, it's how you really are: the things you're conscious of, and the parts of you that belong to your unconscious and you don't recognize (your shadows). This makes it a very powerful tool for self-under-standing and personal development. There are lots of free websites where you can enter your birth information to view your chart. You'll just need to know your day, month, place and time of birth (as exact as possible).

To read the next chapter, you'll need to know your Venus sign in your birth chart. Venus is in a certain Zodiac sign, a certain house, and links to other planets to form aspects. The houses start at the ascend-ant point (AC), which marks the 1st house, and from there, you just have to count the gaps anticlockwise.

An aspect is an angular relationship between two or more planets, and its nature is determined by the degrees of separation between them. They're drawn as lines in the birth chart. Aspects tell us about the link between the planets involved and how they interact energetically. The disharmonious or hard aspects are the conjunction (zero degrees), opposition (one hundred and eighty degrees) and square (ninety de-grees), and symbolize psychic tension. The harmonious or soft aspects are the trine (one hundred and twenty degrees) and the sextile (sixty degrees), and these symbolize fluidity and mutual understanding. The quincunx (one hundred and fifty degrees) and the semisextile (thirty degrees) are neutral or intermediate aspects and represent a certain tension, but without producing a blockage (neither hard nor soft). These aspects are placed in order of importance, with the disharmo-nious aspects being the most relevant and determining, because they are more intense and their experiences more challenging.

Another issue to consider when interpreting your birth chart is that each sign has a ruling planet and an associated house, as they have an energetic connection and a related vibration. For example, Mercury, the planet of communication and the exchange of information, corresponds with the energy of Gemini and the 3rd house. As there's a correlation between the twelve houses and the twelve signs, the 1st house has Aries energy. Below is a table that illustrates this.

PLANET		SIGN		HOUSE
☉	Sun	♌	Leo	5
☽	Moon	♋	Cancer	4
☿	Mercury	♊ Gemini ♍ Virgo		3, 6
♀	Venus	♉ Taurus ♎ Libra		2, 7
♂	Mars	♈	Aries	1
♃	Jupiter	♐	Sagittarius	9
♄	Saturn	♑	Capricorn	10
♅	Uranus	♒	Aquarius	11
♆	Neptune	♓	Pisces	12
♇	Pluto	♏	Scorpio	8

In conclusion, we don't just have one aspect of Venus energy, but many. The same is true of the rest of the planets and the Moon. To interpret all the energies associated with the learning of your natal Venus, you not only have to look at the planet in the sign, but you also have to draw an analogy to the house and its aspects. If you have Venus in the 8th house, you'll find you identify with the themes and characteristics of Venus in Scorpio. If you have Venus in opposition to Saturn, you'll see the chart shows it has a similarity with the sign of Capricorn, so you can also read the section on Venus in Capricorn.

This is a simplification since the aspects between planets are much more complex, but it's a way to make the interpretation of your chart's aspects accessible to you. If you still have doubts, below each of the interpretations there's information on the connections between the planets, because sometimes there are exceptions. Even so, I recommend that you read all the sections on Venus in their entirety, because they all contain teachings that can be of great use to you. Below, I'll leave you an image of a birth chart to illustrate everything I've explained.

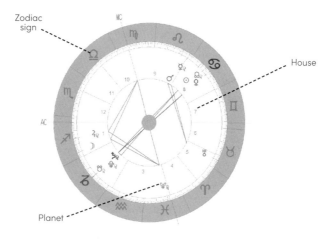

Venus in Aries: The warrior woman

Some days I am more wolf than woman, and I am still learning how to stop apologising for my wild.
NIKITA GILL

Venus isn't at all comfortable in Aries, because she's exiled. Aries is ruled by Mars, a symbol of struggle, effort, competitiveness and self-assertion. If you have Venus in Aries, we could say that you face a great challenge, since both these energies are opposites. However, what might seem like a difficulty at first glance can become a talent with a bit of personal work – and you love a challenge!

Most women have the Venusian tendency to be charming, that is; we say "yes" when we mean "no" and often do things we don't really want to do in order to please the people we like. This is not typical of Venus in Aries, which is her unique gift. She doesn't care about looking good and she always says what she thinks, regardless of the reactions it might provoke. She always gets straight to the point and speaks the truth up front. Some of her talents are her vitality, independence and self-confidence.

I can't imagine her waiting at home for the person she likes to call. She's brave and doesn't shy away. She goes for what she wants, rather than waiting for it to happen. She tends to fall in love quickly and rush into relationships. If she feels the person is worth it, she'll take the risk and dive right in, without considering the consequences.

She's fascinated by anything that smells of adventure, of something new. She's passionate and really enjoys the early stages of a relationship. Her nature transforms when she's in love: she becomes kind and attentive, though she always keeps hold of the fire in her heart.

This lady doesn't waste any time, nor does she exhaust herself with dead-end romances. If someone doesn't live up to her high expectations, she quickly nips the relationship in the bud. If the relationship becomes predictable or monotonous, she'll try to breathe new life into it by introducing something new into the partnership. If that doesn't work, she'll head off in a different direction.

If you have Venus in the first fire sign, then your challenge will be learning to reach agreements, communicate and listen. Giving in at times and being able to put yourself in the other person's shoes is important for a serene and harmonious relationship. You need a great deal of personal space and feel that you can do what you want without being restricted by anyone else, yet at the same time, you enjoy the feeling of fireworks and love at first sight. You'll often experience conflict between the desire for a stable and satisfying relationship and the desire to live free and unattached. Balancing both of these will be another of your challenges.

You adore fearless, adventurous people who know what they want and do what they want. You go crazy for energetic and defiant leaders, but at the same time, you respond to male aggression with anger and indignation, so conflict is bound to arise. There'll be no shortage of heated arguments that end in passionate reconciliations.

Raising your Venus potential

The way to raise your Venusian energy to its highest potential is through movement. Taking risks in your life will make you feel happy. Whenever you tune in to your Venus, you'll feel a passionate, warm and exciting energy.

Throwing yourself into a risky adventure or practising any sport that provides you with an adrenaline rush might be a real revelation for you. Contact sports such as martial arts or boxing – anything that involves competing, fighting, battling and releasing energy – will feel especially satisfying to you. Encourage yourself to push past your limits and surpass yourself.

You'll also enjoy taking on new projects and challenges which you find stimulating, since anything new will bring you great emotional satisfaction. Always keep in mind that if you move forward with an open heart and don't live in the past, you'll feel fulfilled. Although it can be overwhelming at times, being prepared and ready to start from scratch whenever necessary is part of your feminine energy; don't forget that. Any planet in the sign of Aries always brings us the strength we need to break away from the old and dare to make a difference.

Aries is the divine spark, the creative energy, the desire to manifest ourselves in this world. The profound message of Venus in this sign is that we can start anew. Place a blank canvas in front of you, take a paintbrush and some watercolours, and start painting a new story.

The great news is that you can create and influence the world with your own unique style. Let your heart take the lead and let your creativity flow. Being bold enough to realize that what you want requires courage, especially because we live in a world that's constantly trying to tell us who we should be. Who better than you to take the leap into the unknown? Never forget how powerful you are.

ⓘ THIS IS ALSO FOR YOU IF YOU HAVE VENUS ASPECTED WITH MARS.

Venus in Taurus: Sensuality in its purest form

And into the forest I go, to lose my mind and find my soul.
JOHN MUIR

The beautiful Venus feels exalted and full of life in Taurus. Here she can release all her magic, overflowing with sensuality and enjoying life with all five senses. She's connected to mother earth, the physical body and discovering the beauty of life in every moment. She's voluptuous, hedonistic and lives in the present, enjoying the world of sensations. If you have Venus in the sign of the bull, connecting with the present is one of your great gifts. The present is the only place where you truly enjoy the gifts of life. Life has great luxuries, and most of them don't cost money: the luxury of living leisurely; of embracing the one you love; of getting enough sleep; of having free time to contemplate the world and the greatest luxury of all, enjoying being yourself at all times without needing to impress anyone and doing the things that make you feel fulfilled. The shining goddess reminds us that the most beautiful things in this world cannot be controlled or bought; they're already part of us simply because we're alive.

With Venus exalted in her own home, you're undoubtedly touched by her magic, which provides you with charm and the power of attraction. You know how to use your weapons of seduction and project eroticism and a very earthy sensuality. You expect to be pampered and courted slowly and gradually. You have a deep need for physical contact and to be touched and caressed, and sexual experiences must be lengthy and slow.

You particularly like an attractive, well-dressed person who's attentive to your wishes. You're fond of little gifts; a nice present, an invitation to a good restaurant or a romantic getaway will make you happy. You love luxury and comfort – anything that means you can enjoy life's pleasures.

You're not interested in casual, open or long-distance romances; you need closeness and continuity in a relationship. You calmly open yourself to love, and it takes you a while to show your feelings, which gradually grow deeper like tree roots penetrating the Earth. When you truly love someone, you're faithful and loyal to the end.

Once you find that longed-for stability in a relationship, you panic about losing that other person, and you can become controlling. Beware of jealousy and controlling behaviour!

Raising your Venus potential

Venus in Taurus connects you with your value, self-esteem and sense of self-worth. These gifts open the door to receiving all the good things life has to offer. When you feel worthy of all the wonderful things that are to come, you don't accept peanuts and you don't settle for less. You don't have to do anything to be worthy of happiness and receive all the magic of this world; you don't have to pretend to be someone else, because you're already everything you need to be! Abundance is limitless, love is inexhaustible, and we're surrounded by it all the time. You have it within you; you just need to surrender and let it in. Magic cannot be tamed. It needs to flow freely, like a wild river.

Tune in to your body and allow yourself to find enjoyment through it: a delicious meal, a good massage, erotic pleasure, dancing... Feminine sensuality goes hand in hand with the power of nature. Walk barefoot on the sand, watch a beautiful sunset, go forest bathing, breathe in the fresh air, contemplate the beauty of a wild animal and the warm light of dawn streaming in through the window. You can do so many things that make you feel alive. Use your hands: create art, get crafting, gardening, landscaping, cooking or even give a massage.

I don't know if you've seen the film *Eat Pray Love* (Ryan Murphy, 2010) with Julia Roberts, but in the first part of the film, the protagonist travels to Italy and does whatever she feels like doing. She goes out for succulent meals and enjoys every last bite, she prepares delicious feasts and enjoys good company... It almost makes your mouth water just watching it. Every time I see this film, I think this character is the perfect reflection of the hedonism of Venus in Taurus. If you have this configuration and don't allow yourself to enjoy a delicious meal, you're not in tune with the goddess within you.

You have the ability to make your dreams come true, as long as you step out of your comfort zone and dare to look beyond the things you can touch, the things you can see with your eyes. Sometimes, you can be overly realistic and tell yourself that your dreams aren't possible, either because you don't have time, you're too old or you don't have enough money. Don't give up. You're an example of spiritual strength and resilience, and understanding your connection to life gives you the power to dare to go into the unknown and unleash all your creativity.

ⓘ THIS IS ALSO FOR YOU IF YOU HAVE VENUS IN THE 2ND HOUSE.

Venus in Gemini: The allure of intelligence

A woman who reads is dangerous, but a woman who writes is an atomic bomb.
JOSEPH KAPONE

Our goddess is at her most sparkling in the sign of the twins, and she's found in one of her related elements: air. Venus in Gemini makes the most of one of her many talents, namely the ease with which she can relate to all kinds of people. She seems to fit into any environment. She's everybody's friend and loves to go around chatting with everyone. When she walks into a room, she's like a fresh breeze on a hot summer night. No one else livens up a dull meeting quite like her. She finds it hard to keep quiet and always has a thousand things to say.

If you're fortunate enough to have Venus in Gemini you're lucky, because you'll never be short of interest and curiosity. Even when you grow old, you'll still see the world with bright eyes because there's always something new to discover. That curious inner child will always be with you, making people who have lost their zest for life envious.

You're charming, playful and particularly flirty. On a date, you lure people in with the promise that a relationship with you will be a lot of fun, and you're right. In relationships, you want to try everything and experience new things. This deep need for variety and new stimuli can sometimes make it difficult for you to commit to a long-term relationship. This is your Achilles' heel: the thing that scares you the most is being restricted and losing your personal space. You need a lot of freedom and having options gives you peace of mind. It's as if you need a little window to escape through in case the relationship becomes too intense. Don't get me wrong, this doesn't mean you can't be faithful to your partner, just that your challenge will be to go deeper on an emotional level and to take a risk and pursue a relationship if you feel it's worth it.

You're attracted to witty and intelligent individuals; someone who can win you over with their sense of humour, a person you can talk to about anything. There's nothing you hate more in a relationship than monotony and feeling stagnant. If a person manages to keep your curiosity piqued over time, they'll be sure to win you over. Not everything is focused on the mental side of things, however. You enjoy sex, and there'll be no lack of games and foreplay. Connecting with your partner on this level will undoubtedly be important for you because it will help you to focus on your body and escape all the mental activity going on inside your head.

On the other hand, lots of people will enquire about your beauty regime, because no matter how old you get, you always look young and carefree, as if you were a teenager. You never seem to age!

Raising your Venus potential

To tune in to your Venus, you need a lot of activity and a busy schedule filled with all sorts of different plans. Run away in terror from anything that smacks of monotony; you're someone who's going to see change as a wonderful adventure. When your life stagnates, you suffer more than others. You vibrate with movement, dancing to and fro like a butterfly in a field.

You're incredibly versatile and can adapt to any situation. You're always curious and trying new things: that's what makes you feel alive. Plus, you possess high aesthetic sensibility and can appreciate the finer details in many different types of art and creativity. Within you, there's a deep need to understand and express love, not just feel it. Never stop your creative pursuits, be they literature, poetry, painting, film scripts, digital art... Be passionate about reading, gossip on the internet...

You have an incredible talent for communicating and reaching people with your inspiring words. You have a unique way of stringing words together, and you express them with beauty and wit. Don't stop expressing the wisdom of your heart. Do you have a blog? An Instagram account?

Never stop being curious. When something interests you, learn about it. When you're facing a problem and find yourself in a corner with nowhere to go, connect with your Venus. You have the ability to skilfully forge new options in the present moment. You always see a new direction, an alternative to the path that's been laid out for you.

You're naturally sociable, so make sure you socialize a lot. Go out with your friends, chat, talk about your interests, tell them about your life, exchange ideas… Broaden your cultural horizons: cinema, theatre, travel, museums, exhibitions… But above all, enjoy yourself, have fun, keep things in proportion and laugh a lot, even at yourself!

Adventures and new experiences will bring you happiness, and meeting someone who can accompany you on that journey is important. That person has to show the same enthusiasm for life as you do and appreciate your magical spontaneity. If you notice your spark starting to fade and you're beginning to feel closed in, don't hesitate; fly away to a new destination. There are always new horizons to discover, and there's no one better to discover them than you. You're the master of your destiny and you write your own story. Don't let anyone take your smile.

ⓘ THIS IS ALSO FOR YOU IF YOU HAVE VENUS ASPECTED WITH MERCURY OR IN THE 3RD HOUSE.

Venus in Cancer: The sweet side of love

She is water. Powerful enough to drown you,
soft enough to cleanse you, and deep enough to save you.
ADRIAN MICHAEL

Our goddess of love is transformed into a gentle and mysterious woman in the sign ruled by the Moon. She radiates subtlety, tenderness and femininity, and perfectly embodies the ideal woman that every man wishes to share his life with. The longing for love and the desire to find a partner to commit to and start a family with becomes more intense in this sign. Venus in Cancer develops a deep desire to belong and take root in a warm home, one that provides security and emotional well-being. She's very receptive to the energy of the environment around her and won't stop until everything is balanced and clear of negative vibrations.

If your Venusian energy is associated with Cancer, you're naturally sensitive and empathetic, and you have a gift for understanding the emotional needs of the people around you. You exude an affectionate and maternal energy in your relationships, which makes people feel comfortable and welcome. As a consequence, they open up and tell you about their most intimate and painful experiences. You find it difficult to say "no" when someone asks for your help and attention, but it's important that you learn to do so, otherwise you can become exhausted and empty.

Your emotions are intense and you can feel vulnerable sometimes. This means you can come across as shy during the early stages of a relationship as you project your inner sensitivity. You find it hard to express your emotions, and you don't express them to just anyone out of fear of being hurt. The special person in your life will undoubtedly have to earn your trust, but once they win your heart, you'll stick by them with incredible loyalty and tenacity. Beware with your attachment!

You're incredibly intuitive and receptive to non-verbal communication, so it's very difficult to deceive you with words or false appearances. You can be very sensitive if you feel disappointed or let down. You tend to keep your emotions bottled up, which can be confusing for your partner who doesn't understand what's wrong.

You also have a remarkable memory, which is capable of remembering the smallest details of any event. You never miss special dates and can always be counted on for any family celebration. Nostalgia can suddenly flood through you and memories of past lovers come rushing back. At times, you withdraw into your inner world, which is like an inaccessible fortress full of magical and unique sensations.

Sexuality is another way to maintain an intimate connection with your partner. Rather than wild or casual sex, you like to make love wrapped in caresses, cuddles and hugs. In your arms, your partner feels completely safe from the harshness of the world. When you look at them, they melt, because your eyes reflect the beauty of the Moon. You can immediately sense when they're feeling bad, and you know how to comfort them and make them laugh. If they're smart, they'll never want to leave your side.

Raising your Venus potential

Creative expression flourishes with the exaltation of imagination and fantasy. You have a natural gift for storytelling, for relating tales of heroes and villains, of hidden treasures in enchanted cities and incredible, impossible romances. No one mixes reality and fantasy like a daughter of the Moon. You tell magical tales and mythical legends and express what inspires and moves us all. Your stories have the ability to remind us where our true feminine essence lies and thanks to them, we can feel the magic of being women again, with renewed dreams and excitement.

Anything related to protecting, caring and nurturing is the perfect way to connect with your Venusian potential. Why not get involved with groups to support women's or children's safety, wildlife or the environment?

Anything to do with tradition will be a source of enjoyment for you: a wedding, a family reunion, Christmas, an event in town... Being near the sea will recharge your energy, so be sure to enjoy it.

You love to get together with your close friends and play some music in the background. You make a great host, preparing meals worthy of the best haute cuisine restaurant.

It's important that you're bold enough to express your needs and feelings in your relationships. If you don't do this openly, you might end up doing it through manipulation without realizing it. You'll also need to work on your attachments and minimize dependence on your partner. Learn to feel self-confident regardless of the love you receive. Claim your space and learn to set boundaries, especially for the people you love.

Dare to leave the safety of your shell and turn your intuition into the compass that guides you to new horizons. The unknown makes you feel vulnerable and exposed, but if you overcome your fear, experiences you could never imagine are waiting for you. Free yourself from the past and look forward; make your dreams a reality.

Pamper yourself, take care of yourself and love yourself as a mother wolf unconditionally loves her cubs. Find a place of your own where you can lick your wounds and let the light in. Don't let past mistakes condition you; the path you chose can't be changed. Fearlessly open yourself to the new possibilities that are yet to come, knowing that each step you take will create a new story, and this time it is sure to be a beautiful one.

ⓘ **THIS IS ALSO FOR YOU IF YOU HAVE VENUS ASPECTED WITH THE MOON OR IN THE 4TH HOUSE.**

Venus in Leo: The brilliance of authenticity

She has the mindset of a queen and the heart of a warrior.
She is everything all at once and too much
for anyone who doesn't deserve her.
She is you.

R. H. SIN

The goddess shines brighter than ever in the sign of the Sun, where she's rapturously seductive and charismatic. Venus in Leo can't go unnoticed, even though she tries. When she arrives, she effortlessly arouses interest and captures attention. She has a uniquely regal way about her, and she knows better than anyone that authenticity is the sexiest quality she possesses. She doesn't just want a partner to love and protect her, she wants someone who will admire her and put her on the pedestal she deserves. She leaves an indelible mark on her relationships and is never short of suitors and admirers, nor is she short of ex-lovers who still remember her. She loves to conquer, is responsive to flattery and can be somewhat vain, so be careful, because she doesn't like criticism at all. She's easily offended if someone has the audacity to criticize her, no matter how small the critique.

If you have Venus in Leo, you're passionate in your relationships. Your feelings are fiery and intense, and you can go from being happy and joyful to causing a scene worthy of an Oscar in a matter of moments. You feel your emotions strongly, you're passionate about life and want to live it to the max, and you expect no less from your love life. You're searching for a fabled romance; the kind that you only see on a TV screen.

You fall in love easily, and when love walks into your life, you value it and dedicate all your attention to it. You want to commit to someone beautiful, loyal and noble; someone you can enjoy life's pleasures with. You'll always look for someone who makes a difference, someone who stands out in a particular field or excels on some level. You're not interested in impossible love, hidden love or love triangles; you want clarity and to be given space within the relationship.

Image and appearance are important to you, so you'll seek to attract attention with your style, which always exudes a touch of class and distinction. You never neglect your appearance, hairstyle or manners. You're competitive and hate comparisons, but you compare yourself to other women without wanting to, and you can fall into the trap of seeing them as rivals who can overshadow your beauty.

Nothing makes you feel better than a social get-together, getting dressed up and making yourself look beautiful so that you can dazzle at a party. You love organizing events, although you worry that they won't be as spectacular as you want them to be. You're great fun at parties, and you know how to spread your joy to everyone there. You love shows, classy places, trendy venues – and if you can get VIP passes to all of them, so much the better.

Romance is one of your passions; there's nothing like being in love and that love being reciprocated to make you feel special, like a goddess of Olympus. Nobody masters the art of seduction and flirting like you, and you'll win over the person you've got your sights on with your natural charm.

Raising your Venus potential

To raise your expression of the goddess, you need to align your heart and experience the incredible feeling of doing things for the first time, as if you were a child. Connect with your joy and the desire to take on the world. Remember what ignites your passion and pursue it with all the ferocity of a lion. Anything that involves getting in front of a spotlight, grabbing a microphone and having everyone listen to what you're saying will fill you with life. Do you already have a YouTube channel? You could also sign up to drama classes and pursue being a film, television or theatre actress. Maybe you have a talent for being a make-up artist, a designer or a musician. Being an artist and expressing your talent is something that comes naturally to you, so don't forget to give it your all. Enjoy and make the most of whatever hobby you have. Do all the things you love; whatever makes you feel alive.

You have the ability to lead and motivate others with your ideas. Don't keep a low profile or hide in the shadows. Harness your inner glow and dare to share it with the world. Your uniqueness is your power; embrace it.

Don't be afraid to shine, and don't make yourself small to make someone else feel good. You're here to stand out from the crowd and be authentic. There will be people who resent this, but you can't change yourself to make the people around you feel comfortable. Believe in yourself and in what you're capable of contributing to the world. Trust that you're more than capable of doing whatever you set your mind to.

ℹ THIS IS ALSO FOR YOU IF YOU HAVE VENUS ASPECTED WITH THE SUN OR IN THE 5TH HOUSE.

Venus in Virgo: The perfect goddess

Women like you turn winds into entire storms, and yet you ask, am I enough?

VENTUM

Venusian sensuality and charm are filled with delicacy, elegance and subtlety in the sign of the virgin. She's not a chaste goddess, but she does need a certain purity in her attachments. She's discreet and doesn't seek attention; deep inside, she knows that she's unique and doesn't need to prove it to anyone.

If you were born with Venus in Virgo, you're calm and reserved, even shy. It's as if you're untouchable or hard to reach, and this is part of your charm. In your relationships, you're practical and know how to make wise decisions. You don't let yourself be carried away by that inner compulsion to find someone and throw yourself into a relationship without figuring out whether it really suits you. You know better than anybody what your priorities in life are, and you prefer a partner who is mature, thoughtful and always ready to resolve any issues effectively. Nothing annoys you more than a person with no direction who doesn't know how to organize their day-to-day life. You don't like games or emotional rollercoasters. You look for seriousness and radical honesty in your relationships. When these prerequisites are fulfilled, you're a loyal and attentive lover who enjoys taking care of your partner.

You usually mentally analyze your relationship, to the point of obsession. You don't allow yourself to relax. You're very critical and you tend to focus more on what's going wrong than what's going right. In order to obtain your deep commitment, your partner will have to go through some tough tests. You might find a man who looks as good as Brad Pitt, but if he isn't intelligent and can't hold an interesting conversation, you won't look at him twice. You're interested in true love and won't settle for just anything. "Better alone than in bad company" is your motto, and you won't hesitate to break off any relationship that doesn't meet your high expectations. In love, you'll avoid idealizations and fantasies, and your ideal relationship will be real and committed. You're not interested in open, informal or on-off relationships.

When it comes to sex, you're not too fiery and can override your instincts. Intense and uncontrolled passions are not your thing and you're afraid of behaving on impulse. But one thing is certain, when you have confidence in yourself, you can display a fiery sensuality that will surprise even the most passionate of signs. This is certainly a problem for you, as you constantly doubt your beauty and attractiveness. Why? Because your expectations for perfection are too high. This can lead you to judge yourself too harshly because you never consider yourself good enough. It's crucial for you to accept your imperfections and relax your inner self-critic; otherwise, you'll never feel valuable.

Raising your Venus potential

Your Venus feels good when you invest in pleasures that bring you health and vitality. Create routines and new habits and integrate them into your daily life to improve your lifestyle. They'll help you find clarity and inner order so that you can stay aligned with your goals. Get enough sleep, try out innovative beauty routines, drink green smoothies and eat healthily... Taking care of your body and giving it what it needs will feel especially pleasurable, so don't hesitate to follow an exercise routine. Be open to new ways of doing things. Looking perfect and making the most of your natural beauty will improve your self-esteem.

Organizing your home and doing daily tasks will bring you internal balance, and you love it when everything is impeccably neat at all points through the day; when the space around you feels like a serene sanctuary that brings you peace and quiet. Never be without fresh flowers that add a pop of elegance and freshness. When attuned to your Venus, you have a good sense of style and can combine all your decorative ornaments effectively, bringing a sense of elegance and cleanliness to your environment. You have a gift for art and aesthetics and can be an excellent film or food critic. You also love design and fashion.

You enjoy intimate gatherings where you can be the ideal host. No detail escapes you. You also have a talent for organizing large events; you always have everything planned down to the last detail, never leaving a single loose end.

Serving others and being useful in any situation brings you a sense of well-being. You're always able to solve any problem with your intelligence. You love tasks that require time and thoroughness.

Sometimes you may feel a sense of inner emptiness, as if you've not yet found your place in the world. Inside you is a desire to share your gifts and contribute something of value to humanity. That's why you often strive to do things neatly and efficiently, and don't allow yourself to make mistakes. You need to understand that you're valuable enough no matter where you are or what you're doing. Everything you experience has a purpose, and you're in the perfect place at the perfect time for you. Let go of control, surrender to life and let it put everything in its place.

ℹ THIS IS ALSO FOR YOU IF YOU HAVE VENUS IN THE 6TH HOUSE.

Venus in Libra: Eternal beauty

If you're far away from yourself,
how could you ever be close to another?
YUNG PUEBLO

Our goddess of love and beauty is radiant in her favourite sign, Libra. She is elegant and sophisticated through and through. She knows how to captivate with her flirtatious and charming attitude, even without intending to. One smile from her is enough to melt the coldest of hearts. She's a real lady who's considerate of others, possesses good manners and conducts herself exquisitely.

If you're a woman with Venus in Libra, the charm of the goddess follows you everywhere. Flirting is in your blood; you don't even have to make an effort to be liked. You have a natural beauty that wins hearts. Just one little gesture, word or look from you is enough to captivate the toughest of people. You're passionate about the game of seduction, and you're a natural at it. You always make yourself desirable and you know how to arouse interest in a subtle way. You're a hopeless romantic and seek experiences in love because, without it, you feel that life lacks a fundamental ingredient. The problem is that you only feel good when you're in a relationship, which can lead you to neglect other ways of fulfilling yourself.

You're renowned for your indecisiveness in love, and you take your time before jumping into a relationship. You can't bear feeling rejected, and you only dare to make a decision when it's crystal clear what's best for you. Until that point, you might engage in superficial flirting without letting your emotions run too deep or taking sides with anyone in particular. When you're in a relationship, you tend to want to please the other person, and sometimes you adapt to your partner too much, changing your stance because you're afraid that your genuine thoughts won't be well received. You prioritize peace, dislike complications and seek to make life easier for your partner, but often at the expense of your own desires. Remember that a relationship needs to be equal when it comes to obligations and rights.

Although the mental and spiritual side rules over your instincts and passions, when it comes to sex, you're a very sensual lover, and chemistry plays a fundamental role. You're the eternal muse who inspires love and eroticism, awakening intense desires in your lover. In bed, you become a real geisha, an expert in the art of love who knows how to please their partner and turn the experience into something unforgettable.

You possess a natural elegance and whatever you wear, you wear it with style. Your style is understated, and you always dress for the occasion; you never look out of place. What's more, you prioritize good manners and can't tolerate rudeness. There's nothing you dislike more than a rude or inconsiderate person.

Raising your Venus potential

Cultivating inner harmony is part of your Venus journey. Resolve to make your inner peace a priority above all else. Finding that sense of calm is hard work and requires continual adjustment and experimentation, but if you succeed, you'll be able to navigate through any storm. If you're not well on the inside, your relationships and daily life are unlikely to reflect balance and well-being.

To feel good you need to find a healthy balance between your heart and your head, between giving and receiving, between fantasy and reality, between love and professional achievements. You need to live in harmony, so it's crucial that you eliminate negative energies that cast a shadow on your life. Avoid tense, stressful or violent environments.

You possess a keen aesthetic sensitivity and have a natural talent for fashion, dance, decorating, writing, painting... any artistic endeavour that requires you to use your hands. You have good taste and know how to choose the best in any situation: don't think twice about enjoying a fantastic dinner at a trendy restaurant or a romantic getaway to a charming hotel.

Make yourself beautiful, look after yourself and take care of your image. There are many preconceptions about enhancing your outer appearance – it's often assumed that the spiritual path shouldn't be concerned with external beauty, or that a woman with healthy self-esteem shouldn't work on her appearance because it's a sign of superficiality. In my opinion, personal style is something profound that reflects your love for yourself and expresses how you feel. Have you noticed that when you feel bad, you don't feel like dressing up?

Your friends are a fundamental pillar of your life and are essential to your happiness. Keeping an eye out for new trends and finding cool plans to share will fill you with joy: look for the latest film premiere, a play, an unusual conceptual art exhibition or a concert by your favourite band. Be open to meeting new people to develop your social skills.

By connecting with others, you discover yourself and reach your greatest potential. Always prioritize meeting up with someone who inspires and supports you. You have the potential to forge relationships filled with truth and integrity, recognizing the other as a partner you can grow with and walk your life journey alongside. Is there anything more beautiful than that?

ⓘ THIS IS ALSO FOR YOU IF YOU HAVE VENUS IN THE 7TH HOUSE.

Venus in Scorpio: The powerful Aphrodite

She is of the strangest beauty and the darkest courage, and when she walks with intent the earth trembles beneath her feet.
NICOLE LYONS

In Scorpio, our goddess of love is submerged in turbulent waters, searching for a fiery, passionate relationship – the kind that almost leaves you with no time to breathe. She's not interested in superficial flirting, she longs for a high-voltage romance that's extreme, intense and unforgettable. She overflows with eroticism and possesses a dangerous sensuality suitable only for the brave.

Having Venus in the fiery, magnetic sign of Scorpio isn't easy to handle; you're capable of the best things, but also the worst. You don't leave anybody indifferent. In relationships, you don't like half measures; if you fall in love, you either give everything or you don't. You give your entire body and soul, and you demand the same – and if you don't get it, conflict is bound to ensue. You possess an unequalled seductive power; just one look from you is capable of melting ice. You're a real femme fatale who hides her intense desires under the guise of a quiet girl with charming manners. But make no mistake, beneath the surface lurks a dragon capable of setting everything ablaze.

Your ideal romantic situation is to be with your partner, away from everyone else, and simply get lost in the passion, enjoying a connection so all-consuming that a bomb could be dropped next door and you wouldn't even know it. In that space, there's only you two; there isn't room for anything else. When you feel hopelessly attracted to someone, you don't think about whether that person is right for you or not and consequently, you tend to complicate your life. You're fascinated by "bad boys" with a mysterious aura and a touch of danger about them.

You have a keen intuition; you're a sorceress who doesn't miss a thing. You have a sixth sense for discovering the occult and can sniff out lies a mile away. You demand absolute sincerity from your partner and can be very distrustful. You should watch out for jealous and controlling behaviour – sometimes you can get yourself into a state of paranoia!

You ask a lot from your relationships; you have to feel that you're the centre of the universe and the most valuable thing in your partner's life. You know the famous song "(I Can't Get No) Satisfaction" by the Rolling Stones? Well, it seems to be made for those with their Venus in Scorpio. However, you also possess an unequalled generosity, and you wouldn't hesitate to follow your partner into hard times and accompany them in their transformation process.

Raising your Venus potential

You've come to find what you truly love. Nothing will make you feel better than transforming your desire and aligning it with your soul's purpose. When you feel that you have a mission, you become intensely committed and radiate a power that's able to face any obstacle and emerge victorious. You have two options: follow the paved path or follow your heart, even if that feels terrifying.

You possess an inner strength that's capable of getting out of even the worst situations, and you can reinvent yourself as many times as necessary, re-emerging from the ashes. You have the potential to create great things and revolutionize your life. However, you can also crush your own dreams and become your own worst enemy. The choice is yours, my love.

There's no Venus goddess more alchemical than this one. She'll help you see the beauty in the darkest and most painful situations. You'll learn that transformation isn't a safe space, it's a place of rebirth, where you have to be willing to let the unauthentic parts of you die.

You have a great sexual flow, and your second energy centre is powerful. It's important that you're bold enough to express your desires and freely follow your instincts. You can attend sacred sexuality workshops – such as those offered by the Tao of feminine sexuality or the Tantra – to raise that energy and transform it into health and vitality. Your Venus will be jumping for joy!

Everything about investigating the occult fascinates you; astrology is right up your street. Your Aphrodite feels exhilarated when she performs rituals following the cycles of the Moon and the seasons. She loves immersing herself in the mysteries of life and nature, in the myths and legends, in everything we've not been told about our feminine power. Reclaim all the parts of you that have been considered taboo, that you keep hidden in the shadows. Understand that you'll only feel complete if you accept your darkness. Gathering with your friends in a small coven where you can open your heart is pure gold for you. Reclaim your power and understand that everything is cyclical; one day you might be in the deepest depths of darkness and the next, you might return to the brightest light.

ⓘ **THIS IS ALSO FOR YOU IF YOU HAVE VENUS ASPECTED WITH PLUTO OR IN THE 8TH HOUSE.**

Venus in Sagittarius: The wild woman

She wasn't bored, just restless
between adventures.
ATTICUS

Our goddess of love transforms into a brave Amazonian in the sign of Sagittarius. She seeks to remember who she is and what her soul is all about. She's in touch with her intuitive wisdom, with her "creative fire" and her gaze is often wandering into the distance in search of new horizons. She sees all living things as an expression of the sacred and understands that life is full of magic; it can be found in every experience.

With Venus in Sagittarius you're ready to grow and blossom. You love savouring every moment as if it were a true gift. You radiate joy and vitality, and it seems as if there's nothing gloomy enough to disturb your positive attitude. You're a natural optimist, you always see the good side of things, and you know that the best opportunities can be just round the corner. Your feminine strength sustains you through the worst situations because you know you're guided by something deep within and there's nothing to fear.

When you love, you do so intensely and passionately. You value a partner who's fun-loving, enthusiastic and freedom-loving. Someone who make you feel like you're on a permanent holiday. You need a companion who shares your philosophy and lifestyle, someone who's always ready to grab a suitcase and explore new places with you. You might find it hard to stabilize yourself in a relationship, as if part of you thinks that there's someone more interesting out there. After all, the world is so big and there are so many people! One thing is clear though: you don't risk your freedom until you feel that the person is worth it.

You have a strength that simply can't be controlled. At the beginning of a relationship, you're prone to romantic enthusiasm, and the other person will seem one-of-a-kind to you. You'll want them to be a part of your universe, and you'll be eager to pass on your high hopes to them. This extreme idealization causes you to emphasize the good and overlook the not so good, believing that you've found the perfect person. Such high expectations in love will lead to bitter disappointments more than once.

You seduce with your cheerfulness and personal charisma, and can become very popular, with numerous admirers. You're generous, spontaneous and sincere. You have an expansive nature, and love to socialize and participate in as many social occasions and events as possible. You know how to enjoy the good life, often beyond measure. Enjoying sex within a couple is important to you. You're sensual and spontaneous, you take the initiative and express your desires, and you don't like inhibitions!

Raising your Venus potential

Create your own sacred space, where you can travel within and awaken your innate wisdom. If you need to, be eccentric in order to find yourself, go on an initiatory journey, practise ancient rituals with stones and essences, meditate in an ashram in India, explore the mysterious side of life, soak up the wisdom of a master... Spread your eagle wings and soar beyond your limitations. Broaden your vision, go deeper, search, learn, grow, tune into the infinite possibilities of the world. Let your transcendent vision of life inspire people's hearts.

Your Venusian energy vibrates with freedom; it wants to see the world and experience exciting adventures. It longs to run through wild forests, to travel by road to lonely places full of beauty, to get lost in some remote part of the planet, to savour other cultures and ways of life, to meet different people... It screams from within you, letting you know that there are a thousand extraordinary things to experience; don't ignore its voice.

You'll greatly enjoy any physical activity, especially if it's outdoors and, if possible, in contact with nature. Any cultural plan that you feel helps you grow will be a source of joy, and events that allow you to expand your social circle will be very beneficial for you. Dance, laugh, go to parties, have fun with your friends...

You'll come to realize that being stable, static and cautious is like death to you. Make decisions about the life you want to live and the experiences you want to create. Accept confusion and uncertainty; be open to living a life that's fluid and frequently full of excitement and perplexing moments. Ask the hard questions you need to ask and seek your truth. Don't let others dictate what's possible for you. Don't let any fear dampen your fire or rob you of your dreams.

ℹ **THIS IS ALSO FOR YOU IF YOU HAVE VENUS ASPECTED WITH JUPITER OR IN THE 9TH HOUSE.**

Venus in Capricorn: The ice woman

She was powerful not because she wasn't scared,
but because she went on so strongly despite the fear.
ATTICUS

In the icy lands of Capricorn our goddess doesn't want to play games. She takes love very seriously and doesn't take any nonsense. She's patient and knows that the best things in life require effort. She wants to be conquered as if she were a hidden treasure in the mountainside and her hero had to go through the hardest trials to get to her. It's not easy to win her heart. It's not that she's insensitive; it's that she knows what she wants. She's a rock, capable of surviving any adversity, and she won't waste her time on superficial flings. In Capricorn, Venusian hedonism and charm are diluted and put at the service of professional ambition.

If you're a woman with Venus in Capricorn, you know how to pick yourself up gracefully if anything knocks you down. You know first-hand the value of discipline, and you know that without it you get no-where. You're easy-going, and your presence brings peace and order. You're introverted and enjoy solitude.

You hate lack of clarity and people who play with your feelings. Love should have a solid foundation and be something that lasts over time. So, you're looking for a mature and responsible partner who's very clear about things and knows how to keep themselves out of trouble. If they have aspirations and goals, all the better. You'll have the stages of the relationship planned out in your head; a certain number of years for the engagement, then the wedding, then children... You expect them to support your professional goals right from the start, since these are essential to you. You'll be their true ally and the best possible partner, and you'll work alongside them if necessary. Each partner's duties and rights must be clearly defined from the very beginning.

You tend to be overly self-controlled and can be excessively shy and reserved in your relationships. You don't open up to love easily; you need the other person to show that they're sincere and trustworthy. You like to take things little by little, step by step. You like to see how things go, making the necessary checks. Once you've fallen in love and committed yourself, you do it wholeheartedly. You offer your partner unconditional support, and they know that they can count on you in their times of need.

When it comes to sex, you're traditional and conservative, and sometimes you view it more as a duty that comes with the relationship rather than a moment of joy and pleasure. You care about your outward appearance a lot, even though it may not seem like it. You like to give off an impeccable, restrained image, like someone who's far more interested in other things than in being liked.

Raising your Venus potential

You don't allow yourself to indulge in pleasure and enjoyment, tending to spend your time on profitable activities instead. It's vital that you give yourself the space to enjoy life and do those things you love.

Sometimes you find it difficult to understand your true desires and needs, and you often do things by adapting to what's expected of you, by adapting to what's "right" and appropriate, making you act less authentically. This behaviour hides a deep fear of rejection and judgement. It's important to let go of the guilt of not conforming to socially accepted norms and align yourself with what you truly long for in your heart.

Doing something that's both practical and creative is important as it helps you relieve your overactive mind. Any crafting activity will bring you peace and serenity, helping you escape the stresses of everyday life. If you're skilled with your hands, try creating something new from raw materials; for example, make your own clothes, bracelets, ornaments, furniture or restore something old.

If there's one thing you can enjoy, it's reading and soaking up information that might be useful. You also enjoy learning and managing new skills for your business, so a new computer programme or application will be stimulating.

Long walks in nature are a great way to relax and reflect. Conquering a rocky mountain peak will bring you a lot of pleasure. Nurturing practices such as journalling, meditation, yoga, tai chi or any form of physical exercise will help you to focus and centre yourself in the present, so these are ideal activities for you.

You carry within you the desire to grow and fulfil your potential. In order for your Venusian energy to be at its peak, you need to orientate yourself towards success and fulfilment. The problem is that you focus too much on the outcome and forget to enjoy the process. Learning to go with life's flow without resistance and enjoying the journey is something your feminine energy will appreciate.

❶ THIS IS ALSO FOR YOU IF YOU HAVE VENUS ASPECTED WITH SATURN OR IN THE 10TH HOUSE.

Venus in Aquarius: Free love

A free spirit, a creative soul,
a galactic mind.
ASJA BOROŠ

In the realm of Aquarius, the goddess transforms herself into a whirl-wind that leaves even the most prudent of people open-mouthed. She's awfully striking, always surrounded by a luminous glow, and wherever she goes, she never leaves anyone indifferent. She has a halo of irreverent freshness that makes her different from all mortals; she's incomparable. She likes to move at her own pace, without any ties or anything to condition her, always looking ahead. She can't stay in one place for long. She goes where the wind takes her; she's a true free spirit and an eternal stranger.

If you're a woman with Venus in Aquarius, you may not realize it yet, but you have a rebellious heart. Your feminine nature is transgressive and ahead of its time. You don't like archaic conventions, you want to modernize society, you want to change the world and question the rules you consider unjust. You're not taken in by fairy tales. You have a critical spirit that tends to go against the tide, redefining things and looking at them from a different perspective.

You're fascinated by people who go against the norm, and you search for someone who's a friend and companion as well as a lover. Someone you can share your idealistic vision of the world with. In love, you like to try new things and break away from what's established and correct; to define your own rules. Emotions aren't your thing, and it can take you a while to commit to someone. You like to squeeze the most out of life and you'll experience unconventional relationships where you can be yourself and have room to develop as a free soul. You tend to fall in love as quickly as you fall out of it, and if you manage to stabilize yourself in a conventional relationship, you'll try to look for surprises and constant stimuli so that you don't get bored. Even so, you won't want to be glued to your partner twenty-four hours a day; you'll want to make your own plans and disconnect periodically in order to renew the connection.

There's something about you that's unique: the way you talk, the way you dress, your personal tastes. You want to combine a sweatshirt with a sequined skirt? Well, you do it, and you do it with style. You won't stop to question whether or not your clothes are right for the occasion.

Raising your Venus potential

To grow your Venusian energy, you need to explore your full creative potential. You possess a visionary and innovative gift. You have a super-intense artistic side, and your creations are always a bit avant-garde. Don't be afraid of criticism or people's opinions; you have the ability to do things that most people are not yet ready for. Don't let that stop you, don't change yourself in an attempt to fit in.

You're attracted to eccentric things, things that are strange and even shocking to the people of your time but will be considered normal or at least more commonplace in a decade's time.

You didn't come here to walk the road more travelled, live in an ordinary world or spend most of your time yawning. You vibrate with change and unique experiences, the kind that would astound anyone. All you need is to believe in yourself enough to create a life worthy of your energy.

Aquarius always looks forward to the future. Don't get stuck blaming your past and recriminating yourself or someone else for things that have happened. You have the ability to reinvent yourself as often as necessary. Remember that life can be an exciting box of surprises if you're open to enjoying it.

Friendship will always be at the forefront of your life, and genuinely connecting to different people makes you feel great. Your Venus wants to take a leap into the unknown, not for personal gain, but to connect with other like-minded souls who share your desire to improve the world. Coming up with new ideas and opening your social circle to those on the same wavelength as you is always a bonus. You believe in diversity, that everyone belongs, no matter how different they might be. There are many avenues you can explore to ensure your heart is fulfilled, for example getting involved in humanitarian organizations, social causes or other groups and communities with a common purpose; browsing the internet and managing social pages; and making a difference through unique initiatives and developing your online presence.

Your feminine energy isn't for pleasing, complying with or adapting to others; you're here to break the mould and celebrate your uniqueness, not to follow the dictates that others set for you. From childhood, we're conditioned to do things that are socially accepted. We're not empowered by the things we're naturally attracted to. Don't forget that your life is your garden, and you can choose what you want to grow in it.

ⓘ THIS IS ALSO FOR YOU IF YOU HAVE VENUS ASPECTED WITH URANUS OR IN THE 11TH HOUSE.

Venus in Pisces: Sweetness and magic

Throw your dreams into space like a kite,
and you do not know what it will bring back,
a new life, a new friend, a new love, a new country.

ANAÏS NIN

In the sign of Pisces, our goddess dives into the ocean and becomes a sweet and mysterious mermaid lost in a magical world that's yet to be discovered. She'll create an idyllic place for her beloved and charm him with a powerful spell. She always goes where her dreams take her, and when she ventures out of the water, it's not unusual to see her dancing under the stars. She's an elusive escapist, like water through fingers.

Sometimes you'll find her deep in thought with a smile on her lips, remembering a time when her eyes shone as bright as the Sun.

In the last water sign of the Zodiac, love takes on a celestial, ethereal and immense dimension. If you're born with an oceanic Aphrodite, you want a dreamy romance that will envelop you with its magic and transport you to another reality. There's an eternal longing deep within you for a love which comes with no limits or conditions. A love where you can experience inexplicable and indescribable feelings and sensations. The problem with desiring such love is that you'll find it difficult to commit to a normal relationship. You won't be particularly attracted to a solid, consistent partnership with the typical routines and problems. You can fall into complicated romances that keep you in a constant state of ecstasy, but which are never fully defined or clarified. At the beginning, you're naively unrealistic and tend to see everything through rose-tinted glasses. Idealizing the person you're crazy about is very common, and there's a constant temptation to stay in your dream world. If you only see the best in the other person and not the whole picture, you'll be in for a big shock later on. A partner can act as a kind of paradise, a place where you can escape the harshness of the world. You experience sex as something magical, almost mystical… a perfect union of souls that brings balance to your inner universe. During these moments, you lose yourself in the other person. You become one, not knowing where your skin ends, and theirs begins.

Raising your Venus potential

You possess an incredible sensitivity, and you can pick up on things that other people can't. This is your strength, perceiving beyond what the physical senses can experience. You're here to resonate with everything, vibrate at a very high level and vibrate others. You just need to be careful that you don't give yourself to excess.

You have a profound capacity for empathy, a sensitivity that enables you to put yourself in others' shoes and understand them deeply. You're affected by the suffering of all beings, and selflessly helping others will fill you with emotional satisfaction. You'll be very happy to devote yourself to some altruistic work, such as rescuing abandoned animals and giving them a new home.

In the waters of Pisces, Venus raises beauty and artistic expression to a spiritual, pure and sacred dimension. You can express deep emotions through art with astonishing ease. Accept whatever inspiration flows through you, even if it makes no logical sense. You have a gift for inspiring others and touching their souls with your creations. Poetry, painting, photography, film and music are all fields in which you can develop your creative potential. Focusing on something artistic will also be a great way to escape the states of confusion that can sometimes flood over you.

Your intuition comes from deep within, and you need to create a private space to be with what you love and let your inspiration flow. Although everyday life often doesn't afford you the time to take this break, it's important to slow things down, turn down the external noise and align with your inner self. Only then will you be able to hear the music of your soul. Magic is in everything, and you're able to see it in the most unexpected places. Introspective silence will help you decipher the signals of the universe and trust them.

Your Venusian energy is essentially spiritual. It will vibrate when you're in contact with the mystical, with magic and nature. Crystals, rituals, initiatory journeys, the dream world, sound vibrations: all these undiscovered worlds will excite you. Spiritual retreats, women's circles, holistic healing, meditation, yoga, ecstatic dance, tai chi and any spiritual practice that helps you hold the silence are perfect for you. They'll help you connect with the present and feel your body so that, gradually, you can fully awaken to what it means to be alive. Aligning with your deepest self is something that will raise your feminine energy to the level of a goddess.

❶ THIS IS ALSO FOR YOU IF YOU HAVE VENUS ASPECTED WITH NEPTUNE OR IN THE 12TH HOUSE.

CHAPTER 2

The Moon

Our cosmic
mother

THE MOON

Each time you return to your feminine power, you free the women of your lineage who were not allowed to use their magic.

ADAPTED FROM TORIE FELDMAN

The influence that the Moon has had on human beings throughout history is undeniable. Since time immemorial, humanity has looked to the Moon for answers to its questions. It's always been there, illuminating the night sky and provoking a powerful fascination. Its mysterious light hypnotises us as if it were the bearer of a profound mystery that we've yet to learn how to solve. Perhaps because my Sun sign is Cancer, the Sun has always had a strong influence on me, and I've marvelled at her magic ever since I was a child. I recommend that you observe her during each of her mysterious phases; you'll be amazed by the spells she can cast and the depth of her energy, how each cycle is different and provokes different emotional responses in you. Our ancestors observed the movement between the Sun, Moon and Earth across the sky, the cyclical nature of their dance symbolizing the eternal interplay between light and dark, feminine and masculine. The four main phases of the Moon also relate to the equinoxes and solstices. The new moon corresponds to the winter solstice, the waxing quarter moon to the vernal equinox, the full moon to the summer solstice, and the waning quarter moon to the autumn equinox. We know that the frequency emitted by our celestial mother has a significant impact on our emotions. Our instinctive system is connected to the lunar cycles, and we not only experience changes in mood but also in behaviour, depending on the phase of the Moon. Perhaps it influences our mood and energy because we're sixty percent water. Many nocturnal animals – such as certain species of owls – change their behaviour with the full moon. Numerous ancient philosophers studied this and came to the conclusion that the Moon not only influences the seas and crops but also the cultivation of a healthy life, both physically and emotionally. The Moon governs dreams, imagination, the irrational, deep knowledge, ancient wisdom, intuition and the subjective. She symbolizes the invisible side of nature, rituals and magic. She's the queen of the sky, our mother goddess, the one who protects us in our darkest moments.

THE LUNAR CYCLE

Woman's biological cycle is aligned with the Moon, our great ally. The average length of the synodic lunar cycle is twenty-nine days, twelve hours and forty-four minutes, and it has a direct influence on and close relationship with the female ovulation cycle. The Moon has a feminine energy, and a woman is intimately linked to it through her body and through menstruation, which is an organic, rhythmic process that serves as a constant reminder of the complex mystery of life and the creative power within each of us. In the modern world, we've become disconnected from the lunar cycles, but in ancient cultures, rituals based around the Moon were of huge importance and provided great wisdom. In the ancient tradition of the American Indians, menstruating women gathered in a lunar assembly to renew and dream together. It was a time of bonding and spiritual work and a way of honouring their cycles. From this celebration, they emerged fully strengthened; a source of inspiration for their people. Menstrual blood was considered sacred and a symbol of fertility and, knowing its power, they poured it on the earth to fertilize it.

As women, each month we have the opportunity to synchronize with our cosmic mother and let go of toxic emotions and physical blockages. With each lunar phase, we experience an energetic cleansing, and our vitality and emotions fluctuate with its cycle. Being aware of these changes helps us live in harmony with ourselves and our ancestral energy. Lunar energy is powerful and has the ability to pull on our bodies in the same way it pulls on the ocean. We must respect our phases during the month, as there will be times when we need to ebb and flow just like the tides. The changes of the Moon also reflect the mighty cycle of life and death.

The crescent moon corresponds to youth: full of life and great promise. In ancient times, it was associated with numerous virgin goddesses, such as Persephone – a delicate maiden who was abducted by Hades – and Artemis, the virgin of the forests and goddess of wild animals, who alleviated women's illnesses. The next phase brings the culmination of maturity, associated with the full moon. This also has a strong connection to pregnant women about to give birth. Here, the Moon is at its most powerful and was associated with Demeter, the goddess of fertility, controller of the seasons and mother of all living things. She represents the woman as a mother, fertile and protective. The Moon was also associated with other goddesses such as Isis, the Egyptian goddess of fertility, and Hera, the traditional and familiar embodiment of the feminine. Next, the Moon begins to wane, becoming darker and thinner. At this stage, Hecate – the crone – takes power from her hidden place in the underworld, where she weaves her spells. During the new moon or dark phase, the Moon can no longer be seen in the sky. This phase symbolizes death, silence and new beginnings. It's also represented by Hecate, as well as other goddesses who rule life and death, such as Lilith, who's powerful and vengeful; the dark goddess Kali, a destroyer and creator; and a different side to Persephone, who holds the keys to the gates of the underworld and serves as a guide for the souls of the dead. The darkness of this phase allows us to connect more deeply with our intuition and psychic energy, making our inner voice ever louder. Each month, the universe reminds us that new beginnings are always preceded by a period of darkness.

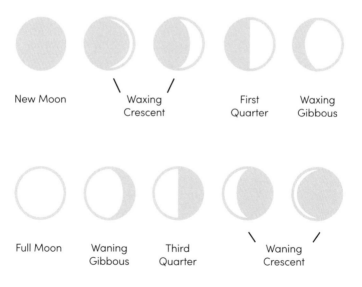

New Moon

Waxing Crescent

First Quarter

Waxing Gibbous

Full Moon

Waning Gibbous

Third Quarter

Waning Crescent

THE MOON AND ASTROLOGY

We all identify with our Sun sign, but rarely do we investigate our Moon sign. Knowing a person's natal Moon gives us valuable information about their emotional world. We can identify someone's Moon sign more clearly than their Sun or ascendant. This quality is easy to recognize because we show it in the first contact we make with others; it's our acquired behaviours. Our fears, reactions and innermost motivations are registered in the Moon. Our past, our home, our psychic heritage, the atmosphere we grew up in and our childhood experiences are here on this planet. Our roots, the clan, the family and any group to which we feel a sense of belonging reside on the Moon. The Moon is the legacy of history, cultural heritage, the family unconscious and everything that stirs up our collective emotions. It holds the memory of our mother, our mother's mother and the different generations. Through our lunar energy, we have the capacity to resolve the emotional conflicts in our ancestors' pasts and take the necessary leap of consciousness for the family.

The position of the Moon in our birth chart – in terms of sign, house and aspects – gives us brilliant information about the characteristics of the protective nest we develop in. It's the first energy we identify with because it's the one that our "first love", our mother, transmitted to us. This first bond with the person who gave us life, protected us and introduced us to new things will determine the way we connect with life and open ourselves to the intimacy of a relationship. The

Moon is constantly changing, just like the circumstances we experience throughout our existence. It tells us how we adapt to change, whether we flow with it or remain forever in our comfort zone. It's our unique way of giving affection, of caring for and pampering others. Our cosmic mother lives within us; she is our refuge, a place we can retreat to whenever we want. It's the energy that welcomes us, nurtures us and presents us with an innate talent that we can use in the world. The Moon represents how we reveal ourselves in intimate moments when no one's watching. How we are when we come home after a long day's work, put on our pyjamas and have a hot cup of tea. In that moment, we disconnect from all the external noise, and we become absorbed in our own thoughts, finding peace and serenity. It's our inner temple, a private space where our dreams and fantasies reside. It symbolizes how we pamper and care for ourselves, how we connect with our sensitivity and vulnerability.

In our mother's womb

The Moon rules the sign of Cancer. Its energy symbolizes the uterus, a sacred place of protection that ensures a baby can grow and develop in a completely safe environment. In the warmth of the womb, the foetus feels totally safe, floating comfortably in an ocean of infinite love, connected to the whole of creation. Throughout pregnancy, the baby isn't separate from its mother. In addition to the necessary supply of oxygen and nutrients through the umbilical cord, it picks up her emotions, attitudes and experiences. The bond between mother and baby is silent, magical, idyllic and overprotective. There's absolutely no separation between the two. The baby absorbs everything from the mother; if she's afraid, her body releases adrenaline, her heart starts to race, and this fear is transmitted to the foetus. Conversely, if she feels happy, she generates endorphins that are transferred to the baby, who experiences this feeling as their own. At birth, there's an abrupt separation from the mother, and the baby moves from a place of total protection to one that is uncertain and hostile. The baby instinctively registers that it can't survive in this unfamiliar environment on its own and cries at the top of its lungs to communicate what it needs. This disconnection from wholeness is experienced as a kind of death, generating a first trauma, a sense of anguish that's only calmed when the baby feels the energetic and emotional connection with their mother again. This is the first major change we must face when we come into this world, and this feeling of emptiness and disconnection will stay with us for the rest of our lives. From that moment, we feel protection and love through lunar energy, which is expressed through the figure of our mother or whoever fills that role if she's absent. The Moon's function is to exert a calming and soothing effect on us. It's in charge of providing us with the love, nourishment and necessary care to guarantee our survival, which is indispensable for healthy growth and development.

The lunar refuge

When we were children, we depended on our mother; when something hurt us, we'd desperately look for her with tears in our eyes, and there she'd be. She'd take us into her arms and cover us with kisses. In our home, we had everything we needed to feel safe and loved. Our Moon's vibration was a place of sacred protection we would turn to when we needed to calm our anguish. As adults, we're still attached to the Moon's energy and unconsciously seek it out in order to feel that emotional security again. When we go through difficult situations that provoke fear or uncertainty, a psychological mechanism is activated, serving as a soothing balm. The position of the Moon in our birth chart provides us with valuable information about the unconscious patterns we repeat over and over again in order to feel comfortable, protected and safe. Of course, as adults, we don't seek out our mother and cuddle up to her, but when we take refuge in the Moon's energy, we are very much like insecure little girls looking for their mothers. We depend on that energy and if we don't find it, we unwittingly provoke it with repetitive and compulsive behaviours. We need to identify these in order for the lunar function to be expressed as a talent and not a regressive pattern.

Our emotional refuge might take the form of compulsive eating if our Moon is in Taurus; arranging the cupboards if it's in Virgo; or partying if our Moon is in Sagittarius. If your Moon is in Gemini, you'll automatically feel the need to speak out when you're afraid, to express what you feel and be understood by the person in front of you. This way, you'll feel calm and composed. However, if you can't achieve this, you won't feel listened to, and your feeling of anguish will increase. You'll often waffle when you're nervous, and you probably won't listen to the other person. This is because you're not trying to have a conversation but simply calm your anxiety. It's important to emphasize that everything to do with the Moon is deeply unconscious, that is, it's often very difficult to catch ourselves in these behavioural patterns. Attachment to this energy must be severed so the necessary process of maturity can take place, allowing an individual life to develop; otherwise, we'll always be exposed and vulnerable to the world, like children in need of love and protection.

Our childhood traumas

Many of the anxieties we experience in adulthood originate from experiences that generated insecurity during childhood. If our family was able to meet our emotional needs and provide us with the peaceful, secure conditions we needed to grow up happy, it's very likely that we'll move through life with confidence and conviction as adults. Conversely, if our home was unstable or our mother wasn't able to give us the time and care we needed, we're likely to experience the world as a difficult and adverse place. We carry the emotional deficits we experienced in childhood with us. It's during this period of time that wounds caused by physical or emotional abandonment may have been inflicted, perhaps by experiences such as growing up alone, without adequate support and affection, due to a specific set of circumstances. To a lesser degree, we may also have accumulated wounds of deprivation from times when we didn't receive what we deeply needed and expected from our loved ones. The Moon is in charge of recording all these memories and archiving them in our unconscious. It represents our way of surrendering the traumas and wrongdoings we may have experienced as children. When a current situation triggers one of those shortcomings or reopens an old wound, we react instinctively and emotionally to protect ourselves. How do we do that? Through our Moon sign. For example, if your Moon is in Aries, you'll react impulsively and aggressively, lashing out at the person in front of you. Whenever we feel threatened, fearful, vulnerable, rejected or overwhelmed by a circumstance, we react unconsciously instead of processing what's happening and responding calmly. These defence mechanisms are a way of controlling the situation and covering up our distress. They're unconscious behaviours that we learned in order to control our environment and protect our inner child from threats. Depending on our Moon energy, we learned to fight, rebel, please, isolate ourselves, control, manipulate... When we use the lunar function in this childlike way, we distance ourselves from our authenticity and true essence. Intimate relationships are the perfect breeding ground to awaken those inner wounds we carry, and as a result, these unconscious patterns we use to protect ourselves are easily activated. Whether we like it or not, in the end, we have to stop compensating and deeply feel what hurts us in order to heal. If we don't, we'll keep entering into relationships that hurt us because we'll unconsciously look for the other person to cover the shortcomings that we've carried with us since childhood.

THE MOON AND LOVE

The Moon is the celestial body of our inner child, which has its specific basic needs that either were or were not met in childhood. It's very difficult for our family to be present every time we need emotional support, so we carry certain consequences of emotional deprivation with us. Our usual response is to demand love and security from our partner; a demand which often cannot be fully satisfied. We unconsciously need this person to give us with what our parents were unable to provide. Whenever we feel insecure within the relationship, this infantile inner child takes over, looking to our partner to give us what we need to feel loved and supported again. If this person knows how to love us, perfect! Everything will go smoothly. But the reality is that the partnerships we form reflect our lunar pattern. We seek connections that are similar to the ones we experienced at home and for our partner to love us in the same way we experienced love as children. Even if this union is disastrous and makes us suffer, it's the energy we're familiar with and it makes us feel at home. We always return to the warmth of the familiar; we become attached to the fire and stay there, even if it's burning us. If our Moon is in Scorpio, we'll view our partner's jealousy as a demonstration of how much they love us. We'll unconsciously associate love with intensity, drama and suffocation. The moment we feel that person pulling away for whatever reason, we'll unconsciously provoke a conflict in order to feel that calming energy again because that's what we experienced as children. Once we have their attention again, even if it's in a negative way, we'll feel safe.

We always return to where we feel at home, to the security of the familiar; we don't understand love any other way. If a woman has her Moon in Pisces and one of her parents was an alcoholic, it won't be unusual for her to unconsciously attract a relationship with a man who, if not an alcoholic, has difficulty coping with life's problems and is unable to maintain a relationship with the necessary stability and maturity. She'll show total loyalty to this person, caring for him and feeling as if she must endure whatever's necessary in the name of love. It's a type of chaos that she's familiar with and considers normal. It's her emotional nourishment, and even if she consciously understands that the relationship is a complete mess, it'll be difficult for her to get out of it. In many cases, it'll only be possible to do so with deep therapeutic and healing work.

Our internal mother

As you can see, lunar energy has an enormous influence on us when it comes to relating to others freely. When we engage with this unconscious pattern and forge connections out of need, we're not free to choose what we really want and enjoy, what really makes us happy. We don't need a father or a mother, we need a partner we can share good times with, someone we can enjoy life with and grow alongside. We don't have to need them like we'd need an oasis in the middle of the desert; instead, we want to be with them because it's truly what we want. They don't have to bring us security, they don't need to fill our emptiness. If we constantly ask and demand, a partner becomes an obligation. A need for constant certainty and security goes hand in hand with boredom.

Love should always be passionate – like in the early stages of the relationship when everything's a game, before our inner child demands their place. Venus needs to be the protagonist in the next stages of love, but for that to happen, we need to remove ourselves from this lunar conditioning. To do that, we have to look within and connect with our inner wisdom and deepest nature and discover our true needs. The Moon is the mother in each of us who instinctively knows what she needs to feel comforted again. It's the nourishment we need to feel confident and, as children, we knew innately what soothed us. If we can intelligently and consciously provide ourselves with everything we need on an emotional level – as if we were our own doting mother – we won't need anyone else to make us feel safe. Then, we can leap into the energy of Venus, enjoying every minute of our existence because we know that there's something invisible protecting us and there's nothing to fear. Our mother goddess is always there for us when we need her; she's part of our feminine essence. She tells us that we're worthy of love simply because we're alive, and we carry all this immense and inexhaustible love within us.

Men, women and the Moon

When we start a relationship, we all show our best side: we're adorable, wonderful, fun, sexy, adventurous... But as the months go by and feelings deepen, especially if we live together, the face of the Moon begins to emerge, with its fears, insecurities, needs and little quirks. Men tend to identify less with their Moon sign because passivity and sensitivity are less accepted in a man, being viewed as signs of weakness. However, this doesn't mean that they don't have Moon energy; they have exactly the same unconscious mechanisms as we do.

Women are good at expressing their feelings; when something happens to us, we immediately call a friend and get it off our chest. Consequently, as a rule, we've always been in better health, both physically and emotionally. At the beginning of a relationship, it's more difficult for a man to deepen his feelings. Nonetheless, although it may seem unbelievable, there's a study that reveals that men are the ones who say "I love you" first. Yes, they might struggle to make up their minds, but when they do, they're braver when it comes to saying the magic words. It seems that we're more vulnerable to rejection – a consequence of being more connected to our Moon. Among other things, we catch feelings more quickly because it's much harder for us to separate sex from emotion. We experience sexual pleasure with our whole body and respond to emotional stimuli. In terms of energy, for men, sex is something that ends with orgasm; in fact, it makes them feel very sleepy. For us, on the other hand, sex is the symbolic start of something, and we feel simultaneously relaxed and revitalized. On an energetic level, we've had that person's presence inside of us, and that connection is maintained after sexual intercourse.

Mentally, we might ignore our feminine essence and want to be totally equal to men, but there's a part of us that needs to feel that person's affection in order to enjoy the encounter more; that part is the Moon. Let's not kid ourselves, no one likes it when our partner gets up, gets dressed and, without a word, walks out the door immediately after sex. Even if we pretend to be strong and tough, we all love to be cuddled and pampered afterwards. In fact, we're far more selective when it comes to choosing a sexual partner. But once men allow themselves to feel their emotions and commit themselves, they become more dependent on the woman, even if they hide it. If she leaves them, the inner turmoil they face is much more intense and long-lasting because they're reluctant to ask for help, among other things. At the end of a relationship, they largely feel depressed, lonely, unhappy and less free than we do. They can go off with their friends, drink themselves to death or flirt with as many girls as they like, but they only succeed in temporarily masking their pain. Women are more anxious about the possibility of breaking up during a relationship, but we get over actual break-ups much more quickly because we're more connected to our mother goddess, so we instinctively know how to heal ourselves, and we can express our pain.

As always, this is a general analysis. In reality, everything depends on an individual's emotional intelligence and level of personal evolution. What's certain is that men unconsciously project most of their unrecognized lunar qualities onto the woman; it's their unique way of experiencing the archetypal feminine. In the early stages of the relationship, the woman is Venus, the erotic goddess who's present in most of their sexual fantasies. When feelings of attachment develop, and the relationship becomes serious, they seek in their partner the lunar qualities they experienced at home with their mother. That's right – as hard as it might be to hear, since childhood they've felt a special connection to their mother. She's their answer to the profound feminine ideal; she's the perfect woman, their first love. How he is with the women he meets in life will depend on how his relationship with his mother was. If you want to understand him, you need to look deeper into his Moon sign.

Bringing the Moon to your partner

Knowing your partner's Moon sign is hugely beneficial because you'll be able to understand them deeply, and you'll often be able to develop a greater tolerance. It's magical because you can give them what they need to feel loved when they're going through a bad time. It's also important to know your own Moon and understand yourself on an emotional level, so you can communicate what you need from that person on those days when nothing's going right. We don't always have to give love to ourselves; it's wonderful to feel the warmth of a hug or see what little things our partner might do for us. Feeling loved is beautiful, and expressing the things that make us feel great is important. Imagine one day your partner is feeling lost and sad, and let's say they have their Moon in Taurus. What can you do to change their vibration? In this case, you could invite them out to dinner at their favourite restaurant so they can enjoy a delicious meal; or if you're handy in the kitchen, you could prepare something for them yourself. If you give them a big hug and make sure to touch and caress them, they'll feel better in no time. If your partner's Moon is in Capricorn, it's easier for them to show their love by giving you something material or helping you with your work than it is by saying "I love you". However, if your Moon is in Gemini, you'll need them to say it in words or text messages.

When they're worried about something, they'll keep themselves to themselves, and you won't understand why you can't solve the issue by talking it through. This is how the main sources of conflict in a relationship arise. First, because we depend on the other person, and second because we stop feeling loved when our partner doesn't act as our Moon demands. That person might love you a great deal, but if they don't show it the way you need it to be shown on an unconscious level, you won't feel loved – and that's when the berating, misunderstanding and emotional distancing begin.

Having compatible Moons helps greatly with achieving emotional stability within your relationship and feeling comfortable in day-to-day interaction. If you both have Moons in the Fire element (Aries, Leo, Sagittarius), and your partner decides they'd like to go hiking in the mountains for a couple of days, you'll think that's a great idea, and you'll have a good time together. But if your Moon is in the home-loving sign of Cancer, you probably won't feel comfortable with this, and you'll end up arguing over silly things. Each partner experiences love differently and has different needs, desires and motivations – both conscious and unconscious. The Moon is perhaps the most important aspect to keep in mind if the relationship is going to last, even if our partner doesn't have a similar Moon to ours. Furthermore, we know that the lunar pattern isn't just made up of the Moon sign – we also need to include the house and aspects with other planets, especially the difficult ones. That's why it's important to work with our own emotional world. We need to observe our reactions to situations that make us insecure, get to know this unconscious mechanism and begin to use our Moon more consciously. Giving ourselves what we need to stop depending on our partner is fundamental and, of course, healing the emotional wounds we carry is a very necessary part of this process. Venturing back into the past to re-experience certain circumstances can be transformative, but in my opinion, being fully aware in the present is the key. It's from that place of mindfulness that things can change. When a situation we're experiencing triggers an emotion, we need to feel it in all its intensity until it ceases. We must avoid numbing ourselves with the habits we've created automatically in order to recreate the lunar energy. However, to do this, we have to be very self-aware.

A relationship based on love has the capacity to singlehandedly heal emotional wounds that occurred in a time we might not even remember. We must truly understand that everything a person expresses is love, or a call for love. A wounded child may behave destructively, but that behaviour conceals a cry for help that stems from a deep need for affection. The power of the Moon is unconditional love, like that of a mother for her child, and seeing beyond what a person is physically expressing. Using love and understanding in a specific moment or circumstance rather than reacting has incredible transformative power. If we only feel loved when we show our best side, we live in fear. If we feel supported and loved no matter what, and that person allows us to be exactly who we are, then it's much easier for light to penetrate our wounds and heal them. A Moon expressed with awareness is capable of transformation and healing, both physically and emotionally – such is the immense power of love.

Feminine intuition

One of the gifts we're given by our cosmic mother is intuition. Deep resonance, recognition of truth, ancient wisdom: all this dwells within you, sending constant signals regarding what's right and wrong in any situation. If you're settled in your mind, you can overlook this innate knowledge. This inner voice whispers to you, always guiding you towards the best option. It's the heart's way of communicating with you. Today we know that communication between the heart and the brain is done through nerve impulses, and there are more nerves going from the heart to the brain than the other way around. Intuition is a feeling that's hard to describe; sometimes it's a vision, a sensation or an inspiration. It most often reveals itself when we quieten our mind and remain present and silent. It appears instantaneously, like a flash. Suddenly, you just know. Your intuition helps you see the good opportunities and discard the bad ones.

If you're not very connected to the power of your intuition, there are things you can do to bring yourself into alignment with it. First, pay attention to the initial emotion or feeling you have about a particular situation. Pay attention to which situations prove that initial feeling to be correct – this is how you train your brain to pay attention and learn to trust the process. By paying attention to your intuition, you'll "tune in" to this way of communication, and you'll be able to decipher its messages better and better. You'll often feel the emotion somewhere in the body, for example a small contraction in the belly or a "lump in the throat". Remember that your feminine intuition is legendary. Keep practising and you'll soon discover how powerful developing this inner radar can be.

I'm sure there have been many key moments in your life when you've had that gut feeling, that inner warning. When we "vibrate low", we're not aware of those signals that are usually so clear. If you reflect back on some complicated romances from your past, you'll quickly realize that your instincts warned you that something was wrong from the very beginning. Our brain prefers to ignore these signals because we're too engrossed in our partner's beauty, but there must have been something that stopped us from fully relaxing in their presence. When a situation doesn't feel right, believe me, it probably isn't. We'd save ourselves a lot of unnecessary pain if we learned to listen to ourselves and be more cautious when we notice uncomfortable feelings.

Awakening your intuition will make you more observant and you'll start noticing little details that other people may overlook. With practice, you can easily pick up on patterns and synchronicities that will become a good basis on which to make important decisions. This profound language also tells you when you're with the right person. If you're confident, relaxed and content when you're with them – and you can also be yourself – you can be sure that there are good things on the horizon. Life is simpler than we think; we're often the ones who complicate it. You possess a wisdom that goes beyond words. Don't forget to use this power.

The talent of each Moon

The Moon is the energy we first identify with. We become so attached to it and it comes so naturally to us that it's difficult for us to recognize it in ourselves. We're used to those unconscious habits that calm us down – so much so that we do them almost automatically. It's for this reason that we find them hard to identify. If your Moon's in Gemini, you might gossip about all sorts online; if your Moon's in Aries you might train at the gym; if your Moon's in Sagittarius you might escape to a European city for a long weekend; if your Moon's in Pisces you might practise yoga... These are things that we need to heal ourselves and feel calm and emotionally contained. Lunar talent often occurs on a regular basis without our even realizing it. Just like the Moon, which has two main phases, we can choose to show the more childlike and less developed part of this celestial body, or raise the vibration of this energy and use it as an innate talent that we can employ on Earth. Just like the fairies in fairy tales, our cosmic mother gives us a beautiful gift when we're born, but we must awaken from our sleep and our dormant habits in order to identify and develop it.

THE MOON SIGNS

The Moon in Aries: Fighting spirit

Being born with the Moon in Aries makes you a true warrior, with the drive and vitality to go out and achieve whatever you set your mind to. Desire rules your unconscious, and it will roar within you until you take charge of what you really want. You probably grew up in a home where you often had to fend for yourself, leading you to develop a strong individuality. You were born into the womb of a truly courageous mother, who you see as an energetic and decisive fighter – the kind of mother who doesn't give in to anything. Perhaps your mother held you to the same standards. Perhaps she was strict and things always had to be done her way, often causing you to feel frustrated and angry. She put her own desires before yours and didn't let you make decisions, and all you could do was fight and try to defend your position. Alternatively, maybe you were already impulsive, brave and defiant as a child, and your mother had no choice but to set boundaries for you. In any case, you established an unconscious emotional pattern of being defensive and putting your guard up at the slightest sign that your space might be invaded. Your emotional reactions are impulsive and aggressive, and may surprise your partner, who might struggle to understand what they said to make you react in such a way. The good thing is that this explosive anger only lasts for five minutes and even you eventually realize that it doesn't make much sense. It isn't unusual for you to quarrel and argue with the people you love, so your emotional life can be somewhat turbulent.

You possess a unique blend of cheekiness, innocence and sensitivity, and you're not shy about saying what you feel at any given moment. Sometimes you don't think before you speak and can hurt your partner, even if you don't mean to. Paradoxically, you'll find a calm person boring because you need regular confrontation. If you don't get it, you'll unconsciously provoke it, because that is what calms you down. Learning to be less reactive and more relaxed is one of the challenges faced by a Moon in Aries.

A deeply unconscious part of you thinks that if you're with someone else you won't be able to develop your dreams and passions. There's a deep-seated conflict between the natural need for love and the need to maintain your independence. In a man, this trait is more pronounced. A difficult maternal relationship will leave a mark, making him unconsciously afraid of women. He may irrationally feel that falling deeply in love will mean he loses his decision-making ability. He associates love with the loss of freedom and will find it difficult to fully commit to another.

Engaging in intense activity is what gives you emotional security. It's as if you unconsciously believe, "If I'm faster than everyone else, I can do what I want and make my own decisions." Your body is often tense, as if you're about to run into battle at any moment. Deep down, you feel that life is a struggle and that you need to do things on your own because no one else is going to help you out of tough situations. Learning to relax, listen to your body and stop over-exercising is a soothing thing to do – if you don't, every now and then, you might build up a lot of tension and explode. Breathing exercises, yoga or any other technique that helps channel your energy is perfect for you. Moving your body will bring you peace of mind when you're not feeling great, so make time to practise your favourite sport, too.

When it comes to love, you need a person who knows what they want, and you won't entertain relationships that aren't clear. To you, routine is a death trap that kills you slowly, so you prefer someone who's able to keep things new and interesting. You don't spend too much time mourning a relationship after a break-up – you hate looking vulnerable, and when something hurts you, you immediately start looking forward. In a relationship, you're in a rush to fulfil your desires and find it hard to wait patiently for things to happen. When you're vibrating low, you have a tendency to go about your business and not consider your partner, so it's important to learn to compromise, share with your partner and let them participate in your life.

You're a fighter by nature; you never give up. If anyone can break their own boundaries, it's you. You never stay stuck in the past or in your comfort zone for too long; you know how to move forward with courage and enthusiasm and make your dreams a reality. Without realizing it, you tend to compete with other women – who you might see as a threat – and they likely feel that way too. As such, you're more likely to keep male company than female. Learning to

trust and collaborate with other women will help you better understand your own feminine essence. When used well, your openness
and honesty make you a great leader, but first you need to learn to
put yourself in other people's shoes and be able to meet their needs.
Be bold enough to follow your own voice, and don't let anyone else
drown it out.

**ⓘ THIS IS ALSO FOR YOU IF YOU HAVE THE MOON IN CONJUNCTION,
OPPOSITION OR SQUARE ASPECT WITH MARS, OR IF YOU HAVE MARS
OR ARIES IN THE 4TH HOUSE.**

The Moon in Taurus: Earthy and exuberant

The Moon is naturally elevated in the sign of Taurus, where it feels
at home. If you were born while our cosmic mother was in the constellation of the bull, your emotional world is serene – like a calm
sea at sunset. There's not much that upsets you. You possess an innate confidence and enjoy great emotional stability. Your childhood
home was essentially a peaceful haven in which you were able to
find refuge. Your mother was protective and loving. She showered
you with hugs, cooked you delicious meals and always gave you
everything you could possibly need. There was always a feeling of
abundance. You never felt that you lacked anything, and could just
let yourself be loved. This affection was expressed through things

you could enjoy: your favourite cake, fashionable trainers, numerous birthday presents... The unconscious message this conveyed to you was that if you have your material needs met, there's nothing to worry about. Money, property and food provide a powerful feeling of having nothing to fear. You're sensual and earthy, emotionally nourished by things you can touch and enjoy with your senses: a delicate perfume, scented candles, a hammock by the sea, beautiful music, a soft bed or wonderful cuisine served with a good wine. You're emotionally connected to everything you hold dear, so you feel a strong attachment to "your things", and you hate people touching them! Your home is your sanctuary, a place full of comforts where you can shelter yourself from the world. You find it hard to move, that's for sure, and you don't like to rush. When someone rushes you, you can get very upset. When you have a problem, you're slow to react and a part of you automatically gets carried away, as if waiting for some miracle to make everything right again. On the inside, you think, "It's okay; if I just let go, everything will sort itself out." You'll often lean on your partner and let them make the important decisions. But once you start something on your own without anyone else's help, you become a rock, capable of solving any problem with strong determination. You have a hard time getting started, but once you do, you're tenacious and persevering, and you don't stop until you get what you want and have it under control.

On a deep level, you're most terrified of change and situations that produce uncertainty. This resistance to changing circumstances can cause you to become stuck in situations that no longer have the same vibration as you, yet you still hold on to them because you have an irrational fear of them ending. You have a deeply unconscious difficulty in breaking away from relationships that have run their course, and you stay in relationships that don't work for too long. When you're anxious, you may turn to food or compulsive shopping as a way of numbing your feelings, so your weight may fluctuate frequently. When you're in a relationship, you tend to become attached to your partner, potentially becoming jealous and possessive for fear of losing that person. You need the trust you have in the other person to be indestructible, and to feel this is a great support to you. What you find most reassuring is feeling your partner's affection through physical contact: hugs, sensuality and caresses are important to you. If your partner also protects you materially and gives you gifts, you'll want to stay with them forever. For you, a relationship is like a long-term investment and should age like fine wine. Routine may dampen the spark in some people, but it doesn't bother you! Making breakfast for your partner in the morning or preparing dinner for your friends at home on a regular basis are things that nourish you. You won't stay in a relationship with someone who's too wild, unstable or idealistic for long, because they'll get on your nerves. You need a partner who's solid, calm and protective. However, you have to accept that things don't always last forever and, as painful as it is, relationships do come to an end. We live in the dimension of change. Life is uncertain. We don't know what tomorrow will bring. Fear holds you back, paralyzes you, puts the wrong ideas in your head and tells you that it's better to leave things as they are – even if they're not right for you.

Learning to let go of what's no longer working for you and changing direction with grace and courage are important goals for your Moon. Your authentic self possesses an enormous inner strength that's very resilient to adversity, and you'll be a great support to people who don't have such deep-rooted toughness. Your feminine essence is connected to the rhythm of nature, the cycles of life and mother earth. You have an innate talent for operating in this physical world and generating resources, and when you throw yourself into the unknown you display enormous creativity.

ⓘ THIS IS ALSO FOR YOU IF YOU HAVE THE MOON IN THE 2ND HOUSE OR IN CONJUNCTION, OPPOSITION OR SQUARE ASPECT TO VENUS, OR IF YOU HAVE VENUS OR TAURUS IN THE 4TH HOUSE.

The Moon in Gemini: Infinite curiousity

Our cosmic mother goes on adventures in the sign of Gemini. She likes variety, discovering something new every day and connecting with people. If you were born with lunar energy in this versatile sign of the twins, you're restless by nature. You're emotionally nourished by curiosity, mental stimulation, laughter and communication. You grew up in a very sociable environment where there were diverse connections. You had a very close relationship with your siblings, grandparents, cousins, neighbours and schoolmates, and they were all very present in your life. Your mother was a cheerful, spontaneous and talkative person, and you could have a lot of fun with her. She was probably an avid reader and passed her love of books and interest in culture on to you. She conveyed affection and emotional support through words and the expression of feelings, but not so much through physical contact. As a child, she taught you that problems can be solved by talking, and when you felt low, hearing her voice would soothe you. She probably read you bedtime stories and explained her way of seeing the world and everything that interested her. Intelligence was highly valued in the family, so you soon learned to speak your mind and be talkative in order to gain affection. You often shared the things you learned at school with your mother, and you were likely to get good grades.

As an adult, reading, talking online, chatting and window shopping is your refuge when you're not feeling great. You find it reassuring to understand why things happen and to search for answers, and you feel that you know a little bit about everything. Although you're never short of varied interests, your Moon tends to be scattered. You learn little bits from here and there but find it hard to focus on one thing. You don't get involved or passionate about anything in particular and often don't finish what you start because something else comes along and captures your attention. You need to explore situations from different angles before making any decisions, and you can become doubtful relatively easily. Extrapolating this to relationships, you have an unconscious fear of committing to what you feel. You're deeply anxious about defining a relationship and will always try to reserve areas of freedom within the connection in order to feel comfortable. You can be fickle with your feelings and change your mind quickly, experiencing sudden mood swings that will drive your partner crazy. It's common for you to embark on a somewhat unstable and chaotic relationship with someone who's little given to emotional commitment. When you're hurting, you need to get it off your chest, and you need your partner to listen and understand. When you're soothed by their words, you feel loved and supported, and your eyes sparkle again. Your ideal partner is open, fun and smart. They have interests, and you can exchange ideas and points of view with them. A person who's excessively slow, stuck in their ways and narrow-minded will bore you, and it probably won't take long for you to move on. A relationship that's too intense and emotionally demanding won't sit well with you either. You like to discuss problems and inject a bit of that playful energy which doesn't take life too seriously. Reality can be heavy and dense, but you know how to live lightly, uniquely and freely, and you need a travelling companion who shares this view of the world. Committing yourself, getting involved and delving into something with passion is your Moon's goal; otherwise, you'll forever be a student who never completes anything.

Our cosmic mother knows that anything rigid breaks easily, so she's given you the gift of flexibility. You know how to adapt to any situation and flow with the natural rhythm of events. You have a huge talent for wearing your heart on your sleeve, putting words to feelings and reaching out to others. You can interact with people from all walks of life and talk about almost any subject.

One of your main problems is that you find it difficult to know what you're really feeling in some situations, because you automatically "think" your emotions. You may put up with a lot of things you shouldn't for this reason, because you only react when something hurts you. When you want to leave a toxic relationship, you find it hard to stick to your decision and can change your mind in a second. Commit to what you feel and what you want! Experiencing states of restlessness, anxiety and nervousness or feeling distracted and talking too much (and not listening) are warning signs that you need to pay attention to your emotional world. You tend to avoid silence and find it hard to stop your mind and simply be. You're always on the move, looking at your mobile phone and chatting, always doing multiple things at the same time, so you can become exhausted. Physical discomfort is a clear indicator of stagnant emotions, so learning to pay attention to your body's intuition will be an incredibly transformative benefit. You don't have to fill every moment with words; remember that sometimes silence speaks for itself.

ⓘ THIS IS ALSO FOR YOU IF YOU HAVE THE MOON IN THE 3RD HOUSE OR IN CONJUNCTION, OPPOSITION OR SQUARE ASPECT WITH MERCURY. EQUALLY, THIS IS FOR YOU IF YOU HAVE MERCURY OR GEMINI IN THE 4TH HOUSE.

The Moon in Cancer: Imagination and sensitivity

The Moon is at home in the constellation of Cancer. Here, you'll find the warmth of true intimacy, of a protective embrace, of confiding in the one you love. If you were born with the Moon in the sign of the crab, you're very sensitive and need to surround yourself with people who love you in order to feel secure. You have a sixth sense for picking up on the energy of the environment around you and you can tell right away when you're welcome in a place. You're so attuned to the energy of our great mother that your emotions fluctuate as much as her cycle. One day you might wake up feeling as bright as the Sun, but come evening, you feel as gloomy as an ominous cloud that's about to chuck it down with rain. Traditional values and family history are very important in this sign and are passed down from mother to daughter. The women of your lineage carried considerable weight in the home and were truly doting mothers. Your mother is a loving and protective being who knew how to provide for your emotional needs without your needing to ask for it. In her embrace, you felt completely supported and protected. Every day her tenderness showed you that there was nothing to fear. She intuitively knew how to cuddle and hug you to soothe your fears. She was the one who understood and comforted you, and you're probably still very close today. The consequence of having experienced such an intense sense of emotional security in childhood is that you unconsciously seek that protection in all areas of your life. You tend to distrust strangers and surround yourself with people with whom you have a trusted relationship. You need to be in safe and familiar surroundings, and you prefer to interact with small, close-knit circles. You're terrified of coldness and harshness, and you fear you may be hurt. As such, you defensively seek an emotional response from people.

For a man, the Moon in Cancer is unusual, because it's very difficult to live up to his mother – his idea of the perfect woman. It often feels as if you have to guess how he's feeling if you want to give him what he deeply wants but can't express to you directly. This is the same for you on a deeply unconscious level: you need your partner to empathize with you and understand how you're feeling without your needing to say anything. You depend on affection, and if you don't receive it, you may victimize yourself and make the other person feel guilty. You may even give in to manipulative behaviour by being unable to ask for what you really need. You give a lot to people and sometimes feel that you don't receive the same in return, so you may become disillusioned and retreat into your shell.

Your inner world is abundantly rich, full of fantasy and imagination. The bad thing is that you treat it as if it were a hidden treasure at the bottom of the sea. Very few people are lucky enough to get a glimpse of it. But once you trust someone, you open up like an oyster revealing a beautiful pearl and exude your lunar magic, which is capable of enchanting anyone who has the privilege of being with you. You give off a warm, magnetic energy, and you're able to feel and satisfy your partner's emotional needs with ease.

You find it hard to open up to a new relationship because you're afraid of hurting your sensitive heart. You may be distrustful, overly protective, shy and withdrawn. But when you gain confidence, you're funny and witty, and a person who can be trusted.

You're very vulnerable to rejection and can misinterpret certain situations, gestures or words from your partner, making you very sensitive. Be careful not to needlessly hurt your feelings! There's a real warrior in you that can fight with terrifying intensity. You interpret events very subjectively and can be very romantic. That's why you can be easily disappointed when a relationship doesn't live up to your expectations.

You can stay in relationships that provide you with a sense of security, but no longer offer you anything else, for too long. If you have to deal with a break-up, it'll take time to rebuild and open yourself up to the idea of a new romantic partner. Building a home and a family is important to you and you'll devote yourself to it. You'll become a wonderful mother.

Becoming a woman who's independent of her surroundings, doesn't put off the things she longs to do and dares to conquer her dreams is your Moon's goal. To do this, you must leave the safety of your comfort zone and face the unknown. Remember, there's often nothing comfortable about the comfort zone. Let go of attachments and connect with your personal freedom. You're immensely creative and your imagination knows no bounds. You're deeply empathetic by nature and you give a lot of yourself to others – perhaps too much – so you need to set aside a space that's just for you; a place where you can retreat and find peace and quiet when you're overwhelmed by your feelings. Create a room where you can be with your dreams, where you can relax and do what you enjoy most.

You're always changing, just like the Moon. You'll have bursts of energy when you shine brightly, and other moments when you need to hide yourself away. Accept yourself in every phase and allow yourself to flow through each of them. Don't get lost in the past and dwell in feelings of nostalgia for too long; remember that magic is created in the present.

❶ THIS IS ALSO FOR YOU IF YOU HAVE THE MOON OR CANCER IN THE 4TH HOUSE.

The Moon in Leo: The soul of a queen

The Moon, the brightest celestial body in the night sky, is bright because it reflects the light of the Sun. However, in the constellation of Leo it seems to shine with a light of its own. If you were born when our cosmic mother was in the golden sign of the Sun, you radiate charisma from all angles. You were probably a very desirable child and for whatever reason your parents were very attentive to you. Perhaps you were an only child, or the much-wanted girl who was born after four boys, or maybe you were born after years of trying to conceive, just when it seemed impossible. Whatever the case, your arrival was celebrated with great joy. You were your mother's favourite, and she proudly showed you off and always highlighted your best qualities. You always felt special within your family, and you didn't have to do anything to be appreciated and praised by everyone. You became accustomed to being the queen of the household, receiving constant praise and attention, but strangely enough your self-esteem didn't grow to be as strong as you might expect. The Moon in Leo has a deep need to stand out and receive positive responses from those around them in order to feel emotionally supported. At home, all your loved ones looked out for you, but when you ventured out into the world, you soon discovered that you were just one of a large group. You had the same obligations as everyone else and didn't receive any particular special treatment.

Inside, you feel different from everyone else. "How is it possible that no one seems to notice me?", you think. As a result, when you feel insecure you unconsciously seek attention, because nothing terrifies you more than being ignored. You're very sensitive to rejection and are easily offended when you don't get the treatment you deeply feel you deserve. One thing I often see in many people I know who have their Moon in Leo is that they're always late for parties, family meals, romantic dates or get-togethers with friends. This is something they do unconsciously to get everyone's attention, because that's all they've known since they were a child, and it makes them feel at home. Yes, it's wrong, but they don't do it on purpose. It's part of their childish mechanism, which is why it's important that they become aware of themselves and start to change these instinctive behaviours.

Importance was placed on success and social recognition in your ancestral lineage, and it isn't uncommon to find an ancestor in your family tree who was distinguished for some reason. The unconscious message passed down from mother to daughter is that not all people are equal. In fact, you were born to a real queen and your mother was a brilliant woman who caught people's attention. Your mama lion had charm, courage and personal power, and you looked up to her. There's probably a part of you, deep in your unconscious, that still competes with her. You may often feel uncomfortable if a friend shines brighter than you in your social circle, even if you deny it. In reality, the person you're constantly competing with is yourself; you need to prove to yourself that you can make a difference. People with their Moon in Leo have a hard time admitting to their faults and flaws and are reluctant to show their vulnerability. Beware of your ego!

However, when you dare to be yourself, you radiate an innate light that's absolutely captivating. Like all Moon signs, you can choose to show your best side or your worst side – it's up to you.

Your emotional nourishment is admiration and praise from others. If you're feeling down one day, getting dressed up to dazzle at a social gathering can make you feel like a goddess again. Moving your body and seeking out experiences that will make you feel alive will also be soothing for you. If we consider this characteristic of your Moon in a relationship, it won't come as a surprise that you need to assume an important place within your partner's life. You need someone who's demonstrative, who's attentive to you and will shower you with affection. You're very passionate and will seek out vibrant, fun times to avoid getting stuck in a rut. You possess an innate sense of personal dignity and always expect a certain level of consideration, so you won't put up with a relationship if you don't feel admired and respected by your partner. You need them to show you they care in order to feel loved. When you feel insecure in a relationship, you demand a lot of attention in order to feel loved and supported again. If you don't get this attention, frustration can build up within you. If your Moon is vibrating low, you can't stand to have the spotlight stolen from you; you need to be the only one standing in it. I've known of instances where a woman with this Moon position was very jealous of her partner's little girl from a previous relationship. Essentially, a person with this Moon sign possesses a pride that's easily wounded, and they can be drama queens who overreact emotionally.

You depend on the image you've created for yourself in order to win the admiration of others. It seems that you can only believe in yourself through external assessment. You're passionate, generous and creative; you don't need to look up to anyone or be told how well you've done to take on the world. Breaking with this stereotype and showing your authenticity, regardless of the effect you have on others, is on your Moon's to-do list. When you stop fearing indifference and put your need for approval aside, you'll let your own light shine and recognition will follow. You're here to live fully. Don't compare yourself to others. The Moon doesn't compare itself to the Sun; each shines when their time comes. You can't spend your life looking sideways to see what effect you're having on people, nor can you keep running away from your potential out of fear of what people might say. You're on fire, and you'll keep burning, looking upwards, aspiring for something better. There's a spark within you that drives you to make your mark on the world. Don't hide yourself away because of your fear of being ignored or disliked; instead, let your creativity flow and show your talent to the world, no matter the outcome.

ⓘ THIS IS ALSO FOR YOU IN YOU HAVE THE MOON IN THE 5TH HOUSE OR IN CONJUNCTION, OPPOSITION OR SQUARE ASPECT WITH THE SUN. EQUALLY, THIS IS FOR YOU IF YOU HAVE THE SUN OR LEO IN THE 4TH HOUSE.

The Moon in Virgo: The beauty of perfection

The order and beauty of the universe is inherently perfect. The Moon in Virgo knows that life and the cosmos are based on laws, balance and intelligence that seem to keep everything in order. However, in this ordinary world, achieving perfection is only an illusion. If you were born when our mother Moon was travelling through the constellation of the virgin, that deep need for perfection dwells within you. You do everything with excellence and care, something your mother instilled in you ever since you were a child. You probably had to develop a certain emotional maturity from a very young age and soon learned to behave well to please your mother. When you did your homework properly, tidied your room and helped with chores, you earned your mother's attention and affection. You couldn't behave like a child and be spontaneous and noisy, nor could you throw a fit, have tantrums or ask silly questions. In fact, it seemed that your family only attended to your childish needs, pampered you and spoiled you when you got sick. You mother was a very forward-thinking woman; she kept everything clean and in its place. She could be a bit obsessive about cleanliness, even neurotic at times. Maybe you were in charge of helping her sort through her emotional chaos, and you quickly learned to be practical and reason like a grown-up.

There are many possibilities for this Moon, but what's certain is that you need to have things under control in order to feel secure. You're methodical and meticulous in everything you do. You take care of the details, always organizing schedules, taking notes and making lists. The worst thing is that you're never fully satisfied with the result. You always strive for excellence, in a way that's almost obsessive. For this reason, you can become very critical, both of yourself and of others. You take refuge in your mind. You need to find logical explanations for everything, and you question what can't be understood with reasoning. Daring to transcend the chaos, to hold the silence, not to attempt to understand what's happening and find all the answers is an evolutionary leap for your Moon. Over time, life will guide you to connect with other levels of reality that can't be felt or verified, and you may become interested in other disciplines that use symbolic languages, such as astrology.

When you're in a relationship, you tend to sacrifice yourself for that relationship – to the point of masochism. You tend to put the other person's wants and needs before your own, and you feel very guilty when you prioritize yourself. To receive affection and feel emotionally supported, you need to help your partner and feel useful, but you can fall into the trap of doing too much for them and too little for yourself. Without realizing it, you may end up organizing their life, and then one of two things might happen: they might feel very comfortable with the situation and take advantage, or they might flee in terror and feel like you're controlling them too much. You're afraid to impose your wishes and assert what you need, especially if it deeply contradicts with what that person expects from you. It's so important to say "no" when you need to and to set boundaries! If you don't, you can give too much and end up totally drained.

You often suffer in silence and don't allow your emotions to bubble over. You rationalize your feelings and tend to control your emotions, and you don't express how you feel – often you don't even know yourself. It isn't uncommon to find yourself organizing and cleaning the house when you have a problem as a way of sorting out your inner world. When your inner child can't take it anymore, your emotions might manifest as physical symptoms and make you unwell; it's an unusual way of asking for the love you need. Connecting with your traumas and allowing yourself to feel them will be soothing for you. Express your rage, your anger. Let yourself lose control. Let go, free yourself, untie yourself, think about you. Accept your chaos unconditionally. Start giving yourself what you want and need, even if no one agrees with it. Always be your true self. It's not about being perfect, it's about being authentic.

We all have a low tolerance for unforeseen events and uncertainty, but it's not good to become obsessed with having everything planned and under control. Going with the flow, not being too rigid and becoming more flexible is an art. Remember that the good things in life cannot be controlled. Of course, you need to follow the daily routines that make you feel good, such as your need for rest, exercise and a healthy diet. Living in a calm environment in a space that's clean and clear of objects and noise will help you find inner balance. Letting go of negative vibrations and thoughts and replacing them with good feelings is especially important for you, because you tend to worry too much. To achieve this, engage in any ritual that purifies the mind and body and brings you peace, serenity and full acceptance of the present moment.

❶ THIS IS ALSO FOR YOU IF YOU HAVE THE MOON IN THE 6TH HOUSE OR VIRGO IN THE 4TH HOUSE.

The Moon in Libra: Justice and equality

The lunar energy is filled with subtlety and harmony in the extraverted sign of Venus. Being born with the Moon in Libra means you possess charm and refinement when it comes to connecting with others. As a child, you learned that tantrums and sulking got you nowhere and that to get your mother's affection, you had to have good manners and ask for things politely and respectfully. She was probably very sociable, a great hostess who always greeted guests with a charming smile. She might have worried too much about what people said and likely always maintained good manners and a perfect image. She wasn't particularly demonstrative with her affection, but she was reasonable and talkative. You learned the gift of diplomacy from her and in your relationships, you always seek to reconcile and reach agreements.

There's a toxic charm about this Moon, which is never angry and always keen to please. You often find it difficult to assert yourself and, even if you're absolutely right, you prioritize peace, choosing to keep quiet about what you really think or feel about a situation. You'll often tell a little lie in order not to hurt your partner's feelings, as you can't bear to do or say anything that would cause the slightest displeasure. If you do, you'll immediately try to make up for it and keep the peace. This may seem deceptive or hypocritical, but in reality it's a deep empathic ability that leads you to constantly seek harmony with the person or place you're in. You unconsciously try to avoid conflict, preferring understanding and dialogue. You don't feel comfortable when there's emotional distance between people. You're naturally good at making connections with people; you always try to listen and empathize. However, sometimes discussions are necessary, they help us be honest, explore our desires and uncover what's not working in the relationship. How can we explore exactly what's wrong if we avoid confrontation?

You need company at all times, because you have an irrational fear of loneliness. You love being in love and when you think you've found "the one" you let yourself get carried away, as if nothing else exists. Your friends might ask you to hang out, but you've already chosen your main priority. Having a partner to share your life with is what nourishes you emotionally. You're fascinated with connecting to that person, with having the same tastes, with joining forces. You normally want the decisions you make in life to be made through mutual agreement. The problem is that you need to be in a relationship to be happy, and this can lead to emotional dependency. You might stay in a relationship that doesn't fulfil you for too long, maintaining it as a purely formal and aesthetic bond that's just for show. When faced with a break-up, you may feel as if your very existence is threatened. This might sound like an exaggeration, but you feel it on an instinctive level. It's essential that you learn to be happy on your own, alone with yourself and doing the things you love most.

You're charming and considerate of other people's opinions, and often make yourself available for whatever they need. You know exactly how to make your partner happy, and you accompany them in whatever they want to do, often ignoring your own wishes and needs in the process. Discovering what you really want and expressing it, even if it contradicts what your partner wants, is the evolutionary leap your Moon needs to take. It's important to learn to say "no" and to set your boundaries. Being firm, even if the other person disagrees, is necessary for a healthy, equal relationship. Otherwise, you'll often give "too much" and probably not get as much in return. Other times, your inner vigilante will emerge and you'll demand the Libran qualities of equality and balance, leaving your partner open-mouthed at the unexpected strong reaction. Remember that you shouldn't lose yourself in a relationship: your whole life can't revolve around that one person. There are other things that can fulfil you in the same way, so make sure to explore them.

Emotional outbursts are unusual for you, and you find it difficult to express your feelings spontaneously. You unconsciously adapt to your surroundings, always behaving in a way that's appropriate for the situation and keeping up appearances. Even if you feel like you need to smash a plate and scream like crazy, you don't allow yourself to do so if it's not appropriate. You think, "they'll think I'm mad!" Give yourself permission to be hysterical once in a while: you'll find it's particularly refreshing. Be honest and tell the truth, no matter what. The things we don't say create a shadow, an ugly energy that slowly erodes a relationship. Eventually, everything that builds up explodes and then ugly, hurtful things are said.

If there's one thing that gets you fired up and feeling like you might explode, it's injustice. You instinctively defend vulnerable people who can't defend themselves. It's not unusual for you to fight for noble causes, such as women's rights or animal rights, or even to have become a vegan out of conviction.

ⓘ THIS IS ALSO FOR YOU IF YOU HAVE THE MOON IN THE 7TH HOUSE OR IN CONJUNCTION, OPPOSITION OR SQUARE ASPECT WITH VENUS. EQUALLY, THIS IS FOR YOU IF YOU HAVE VENUS OR LIBRA IN THE 4TH HOUSE.

The Moon in Scorpio: Swimming in the darkness

This is one of the most complex Moons to experience. If you were born when the Moon was bathing in the depths of the constellation of Scorpio, you burn with deep passion and desire. Your mother may have had a complicated pregnancy, during which she felt fear, had physical complications or experienced a traumatic event. I know of mothers who had several previous miscarriages and the baby developed in the womb with that knowledge of pain and death. Another woman I spoke with explained that her mother almost bled to death after giving birth. Somehow, the mother placed this fear onto the baby, making the child the centre of her world. She could be over-protective and took care of everything. She went out of her way for her child, as if she were an extension of herself. She attended to her little girl's every need, and subsequently reinforced her dependence on her child and kept her close at all times. She gives her daughter every ounce of her love, but unconsciously expects a lot in return. She's a demanding, possessive mother, and may even make the final decision in all aspects of her child's life without considering that her daughter's wants and needs might differ from her own. She decides what after-school classes she attends, supervises her friendships and organizes her parties. An extreme manifestation of this can be the suffocating mother who completely invades her child's space and leaves them with no privacy. She doesn't do this maliciously: she simply wants to give them all the things she never had in her own childhood. The child learns from a very early age that in order to be met with love, they must let themselves be trapped by their mother and not put up any sort of resistance. They feel that if they deviate from her guidelines, they'll automatically lose their mother's affection. We already know that almost every mother loves their children unconditionally, but everything concerning the Moon in Scorpio happens on a level that's extremely difficult to identify.

There are many possibilities for this Moon sign, but if you were born with your Moon in Scorpio, you unconsciously seek very intense relationships, and you'll only feel loved if you allow yourself to get caught in the web. A part of you will want to run away, but you'll find that if you do, you can't find an emotional refuge. You may take years to commit to someone emotionally for fear of losing your identity within an all-consuming partnership. Your partner will encompass many aspects of your life and there won't be much room for personal freedom. You'll make decisions together as one and there'll be no secrets between you. On an unconscious level, you associate love with pain, drama, a sense of suffocation and lack of space. If there's no jealousy or demands from your partner, you won't feel loved. "Superficial" relationships simply don't interest you, you vibrate when transformation and passion are almost taken to the extreme. When you're insecure, you can become possessive, demanding and even manipulative, because you need to feel that there's no room for doubt within your relationship. Paradoxically, you refuse to let your partner become too intense and possessive of you. As you can see, your Moon is contradictory, and so is your emotional world, which often experiences extreme ups and downs. You have a strong need to express your deep and powerful emotions, but another part of you needs to control them for fear of the effect they may have. You over-protect your vulnerability, and sometimes don't say what you feel but still expect the other person to give you what you profoundly expect. If they don't, the war is on. You possess a unique intuition, a vision that perceives beyond experience and is capable of uncovering people's true intentions, things that are false and superficial and even the most well-hidden of mysteries. I doubt there's anyone who could lie to your face.

You have an inner strength and a capacity for regeneration that will enable you to face the most difficult situations and emerge stronger. Like a phoenix rising from the ashes, you'll have to hit rock bottom and cause destruction before you can experience the light of a new consciousness. It's when it gets really dark that you can see the true light that dwells within you.

You're distrustful by nature and when you feel insecure you look for conflicts where there are none. I know of a person with this Moon who, whenever something happens in her daily life that makes her uneasy, seeks to calm herself down by unconsciously provoking her partner's anger with words, hurtful jokes or inappropriate behaviour. Once an argument breaks out, the other person is left devastated, but she feels completely calm. You'll understand how important it is to be aware of these childish behaviours in order to have healthy relationships. Learning to relax, trust and simply enjoy yourself with that person is key to getting out of the toxic dynamic that this Moon demands.

When you fall in love, you're incredibly loyal and committed, and would never cheat on your partner. However, you must avoid making romance the centre of your world and making that person the most important thing in your life. Loving without possessing, invading or depending is a long and difficult journey, but it's so magical to experience freedom as a couple! It's good to have space where you can each have secrets or unspeakable longings, where you can explore the things that make you happy without the need for the other person's participation. You can love them like you love the Sun on a summer afternoon – you don't want to possess them; you just want to enjoy their light and warmth. To achieve this, you must be willing to let the other person leave whenever they please. That's magic and true love.

❶ THIS IS ALSO FOR YOU IF YOU HAVE THE MOON IN THE 8TH HOUSE OR IN CONJUNCTION, OPPOSITION OR SQUARE ASPECT WITH PLUTO. EQUALLY, THIS IS FOR YOU IF YOU HAVE PLUTO OR SCORPIO IN THE 4TH HOUSE.

The Moon in Sagittarius: The love of an adventure

The Moon expands and fills with joy and optimism on its journey through Sagittarius. Our great mother knows that everything has meaning and that we just need to let go and learn to flow with the river of life. Being born with your Moon in the sign of the archer makes you curious to expand your horizons and push your limits. Your intuition guides you and helps you overcome any obstacles. It may seem as if you're lucky, but the reality is that, deep down, you just believe in the infinite possibilities of the world.

Your mother has joy, charisma and people skills. She taught you that everything's okay and there's nothing to fear. She was probably a person with ideals, with religious or spiritual principles, and she passed on her profound wisdom to you. When you displayed pessimism and sadness, she was quick to stop you indulging in such destructive emotions. She knows that the best way to navigate life is to be positive and trust that there's something higher guiding our steps. Your parents were generous and tolerant, and helped you to trust your intuitions and think for yourself. At home, you'd been free to move around and had your own space to do what you wanted to do. It's very likely that you had contact with people from foreign countries or travelled a lot, or that someone in your family was a scholar, professor or teacher in some field. This home gave you an innate sense of self-confidence and taught you how to take the necessary steps to bring your ideas to life.

You always feel free to do what you feel like doing, and you don't stop to analyze the pros and cons. You don't let yourself doubt things; instead, you let yourself be carried away by blind optimism, and you're often disappointed when things don't turn out as you expected. You look for answers that assign a profound meaning to everything that happens to you, though the negative of this is that you justify the unjustifiable too often. You're a real expert at downplaying problems; you might even deny the conflicts of reality that you find too difficult to face, or avoid them altogether by distancing yourself through having fun or travelling. Through disappointment, you'll learn to deal with difficult situations and see the truth of what's going on so that you can make the necessary changes.

You're a traveller by nature; nothing makes you feel better than packing your suitcase and flying to some distant part of the world. Discovering other countries, experiencing other cultures and getting lost in the world is where you feel at home, as if you're back in the womb. You need to keep your horizons broad, explore new places and connect with people who are different from you. With this lunar position, you're driven to set new goals, learn metaphysical things, find higher purpose and expand your consciousness. You love to share the truth and wisdom you've acquired over the years. You may well have a natural gift for inspiring others to be the best they can be.

Your passionate belief in your truth can lead you to quickly dismiss other ideas that may contradict your point of view. You don't like criticism and may be offended if someone questions your beliefs.

But remember that truth has many sides and there are many ways of approaching it, so understanding other points of view will only enrich your vision.

You can't stand limits and restrictions. You're always ready to renew your life, tear down any wall and jump over any obstacle that tries to hold you back. You can be very idealistic, and this carries through into your love life. You need a person who shares your transcendent vision of life and is always ready to embark on a new adventure with you. When you fall in love, you have a tendency to idealize too much, and you can be disappointed when that person doesn't live up to your deepest expectations. Facing the pain of reality and holding on to disappointment is necessary; otherwise, you'll always avoid making decisions. You'll justify everything in the name of love and may maintain relationships that aren't right for you.

You're passionate, fun and inspiring. If anyone believes in the impossible, it's you. You can't be with someone who's pessimistic, boring and overly realistic for long. Their words will come as a shock to you, and it won't be long before you hit the road and run somewhere else. In a relationship, you like to know that you have your own space and are free to do the things you like to do without having to put up with anyone's demands. Part of you might fear commitment. You hate being stuck in a routine for too long and will periodically need to escape. You'll only settle down in a long-term relationship with someone who brings positive things into your life, with someone who you can grow and evolve with. However, you'll need to make it clear to the other person that you are a wild soul who can never be completely tamed.

ℹ THIS IS ALSO FOR YOU IF YOU HAVE THE MOON IN THE 9TH HOUSE OR IN CONJUNCTION, OPPOSITION OR SQUARE ASPECT WITH JUPITER. EQUALLY, THIS IS FOR YOU IF HAVE JUPITER OR SAGITTARIUS IN THE 4TH HOUSE.

The Moon in Capricorn: Making dreams a reality

In the cold and distant lands of Capricorn, the Moon is in exile. Our great mother needs a warm, intimate and cozy environment, but here she finds only coldness and loneliness. Being born with the Moon in this sign gives you an independent and reserved nature. As a child, you already exuded a halo of self-sufficiency and maturity, like an old soul with deep wisdom. From an early age, you often had to manage on your own because your mother worked a lot and couldn't give you all the attention you needed. Perhaps she wasn't very demonstrative with her affections or was going through difficult times. It's very common to have been born into an environment where there were economic restrictions. If you did have material abundance, there were strict rules and a lot of demands to comply with your obligations. What matters to your family is what you do in life, what you can achieve through hard work, how far you're able to go. There were times during your childhood when you asked for love and attention but you didn't receive it, so you slowly got used to not being too demanding or too much of a nuisance at home. Your mother leaned on you when she felt overwhelmed and assigned you chores, so you often had to take care of a lot of things that weren't the responsibility of someone your age. You felt like you only earned her love and attention when you did things right and did what she told you to do.

In some cases, those with their Moon in Capricorn experience a lot of loneliness and a sense of abandonment that might leave a strong unconscious mark. You've learned to disconnect from your emotions, reject your feelings and not need affection. When a painful event happens, such as a break-up, you don't allow yourself to feel for too long; you might not even feel anything at all. You tend to withdraw inward and lick your wounds in solitude. You're not easily overwhelmed by life events, and they don't have the same impact on you as they do on other people. Work is an emotional bunker where you can take refuge from pain. You're the cornerstone of your family and friends, who lean on you and ask for your help. To get affection, you're often burdened with commitments and responsibilities from others and paradoxically, you always end up complaining that you're the one who has to take care of everything. Your desire to depend on no one sometimes results in your needing help and support, but you don't ask for it. Instead, you carry around an uncomfortable feeling of frustration and loneliness.

You over-adapt to social norms and wear a mask of good behaviour, putting a limit on the free expression of your most authentic self. You can be extremely critical and demanding of yourself, even carrying a sense of guilt when you fail to meet others' standards or expectations. You put duty before your heart's desires and sacrifice your dreams to achieve what's expected of you. If you look back over your life, you'll see that all too often, you've been where you felt you should have been rather than where you really wanted to be.

You don't get involved in a relationship unless you feel it has a promising future. You're demanding, and few people touch your heart. You're not very romantic, and you're practical and clever in love. People with Peter Pan syndrome – who seem like they'll be teenagers forever – might seem charming and exciting to some women, but they don't appeal to you at all, nor are you particularly interested in starving artists who live in attics and do crazy things in pursuit of their crazy dreams. You're interested in achievers, people who know how to pursue success and professional goals with ambition and a cool head. Because of this, you might be single for a long time, patiently waiting for the right partner to come along.

You're very distrustful and need a lot of reassurance before you open yourself up to a new relationship. You unconsciously protect yourself by wearing a mask of self-sufficiency and coldness when you feel insecure in front of someone you like, which can be disconcerting. At the beginning of a relationship, you prefer to take things slowly and rely on facts rather than on empty words or hollow hopes. You don't get caught up in unbridled passions and can separate yourself from intense emotions with the impartiality of a scientist. However, behind that detached and distant façade lies a vulnerable child in need of love, even if you don't allow yourself to ask for it. Unconsciously, you're still holding on to the memory of the frustration you felt when you asked for affection and didn't receive it. When you enter the turbulent waters of your emotions, you feel that you lose yourself. Deepening your feelings, embracing and expressing affection, trusting, letting yourself feel your emotions, understanding yourself, going with the flow... This is what people with your Moon sign need to work on. You don't have to prove anything or do anything specific to earn affection. You forget about yourself too often; it's important that you learn to listen to yourself and give yourself what you deeply need. Your Moon has gifted you with the possibility of achieving true emotional freedom, but first you must dare to connect with your feelings and express them, otherwise negative emotions can build up within you and cause you various physical problems. Take care of yourself as much as you can.

ⓘ THIS IS ALSO FOR YOU IF YOU HAVE THE MOON IN THE 10TH HOUSE OR IN CONJUNCTION, OPPOSITION OR SQUARE ASPECT WITH SATURN. EQUALLY, THIS IS FOR YOU IF YOU HAVE SATURN OR CAPRICORN IN THE 4TH HOUSE.

The Moon in Aquarius: The magic of freedom

In the constellation of Aquarius, our cosmic mother leaves the comfort of her daily world to enter an unfamiliar reality. She seems to be suspended in a different dimension, as if lost in the vastness of the universe. Here, she feels far away from everything and, although she's sometimes afraid, she experiences the magic of true freedom. If you were born when the Moon was in Aquarius, you have a rebellious spirit and love to be free more than anything else. Your forward-thinking soul was born before its time; in fact, you sometimes feel so out of place it's as if you came from a future society and don't belong here.

Ever since you were a child you felt different from everyone else, like you didn't fit in anywhere. You probably felt like some sort of alien within your own family. Your mother was probably a woman ahead of her time, with innovative ideas, alternative opinions and a very open mind. Maybe she was bohemian, engaged in some counter-cultural movement, a hippie or perhaps just a bit wild. You likely considered her more of a friend than a mother. She was a mother who was distant yet close, simultaneously absent and present. Your home environment was probably unconventional and a lot of different people came and went through the front door. Somehow, she broke with the traditions of the past and your family life had an eccentric feel about it. Your childhood was a time of disruption and unexpected circumstances: sudden moves, new countries, an unexpected divorce... Even your mother experienced various problems and exceptional circumstances that often prevented her from being with you. You grew up trying to get used to the changes and disruption in your home life, and became detached to prevent yourself from suffering. Emotional support was unpredictable and inconsistent, so you learned to find support from others around you, such as friends or grandparents, in order to cope. You may even have experienced a traumatic event that generated a great deal of distress, and the emotional abandonment you felt may have left a deep wound. These events taught you that attachment and love can disappear in the blink of an eye.

As an adult, your chosen emotional refuge is simply to not feel; to know that you can do what you please without being limited or defined by anything. You don't tolerate emotional intensity, you detach yourself from your feelings and prefer to be objective and analyze what's happening to you on a mental level, from a certain distance.

You love relating to diverse groups of people, and you'll have no shortage of friends and colleagues you can have a good time and share ideas and interests with. However, complications arise when it comes to love. True intimacy and intense feelings make you uneasy, simply because you don't know how to manage everything that goes on between two people when they love each other. Deep down, there's a fear that this affection will be disrupted again, and you'll be left abandoned, suspended in a void, suffering from an uncontrollable anguish. Instead, you prefer to control, flee, establish distance, sabotage and set boundaries when that person gets too close. You can often be passionate and giving, and you can also be distant and impersonal. This ends up disconcerting the other person and spoiling the relationship. As soon as you feel hurt and rejected, you disconnect from your emotions and become cold, indifferent and even cruel, as if you feel nothing at all. But the truth is that you're hurting, and avoiding those feelings of hurt can cause them to build up and eventually explode, materializing into impulsive actions, bizarre reactions and radical changes that leave everyone shocked.

During certain phases of your life, you may prefer free and uncommitted relationships, because nothing makes you more uneasy than an all-absorbing relationship. That doesn't mean that you don't fall in love – you might do so with sudden enthusiasm. In fact, you've had your fair share of crushes, and you might have numerous romances with very diverse and exciting people. The problem is that you fall out of love just as quickly. You dislike excessive demands and hate being pressured to define a relationship that's not clear to you. You have a rebellious temperament and don't like having things imposed on you, and this can make you inflexible. You need to find a person who's original and understands your unique vision of life, who shares your idealism and your social and cultural concerns. Your spirit is transgressive and brilliant, and you tend to rise above family expectations, roles and stereotypes and stay focused on the future. You possess an incredible creativity that helps you stand out from the crowd, often without your realizing it. You're easily bored and need to switch things up every now and then to keep life exciting and fresh. The goal for your Moon sign is to open your heart to the person you love without losing any of yourself. Our cosmic mother encourages you to respect your authentic essence and your considerable need for space, but she also wants you to trust in love and be brave enough to hold on to those feelings that develop for that special person.

❶ THIS IS ALSO FOR YOU IF YOU HAVE THE MOON IN THE 11TH HOUSE OR IN CONJUNCTION, OPPOSITION OR SQUARE ASPECT WITH URANUS. EQUALLY, THIS IS FOR YOU IF YOU HAVE URANUS OR AQUARIUS IN THE 4TH HOUSE.

The Moon in Pisces: A journey in dreamland

The Moon sails the ocean of Pisces, lost in the vastness of the mystery of life. She's the great cosmic and universal mother who's always there to protect you. The one you can turn to when you feel helpless. In this sign, her archetypal influence is colossal. Whenever you feel afraid, she envelops you in her magic, transporting you to a dreamland where anything is possible. To be born when the Moon was swimming in this sign of the Zodiac is a powerful gift that must be handled wisely; otherwise, you might get lost in an elaborate labyrinth. Like the Moon, your mother was overprotective and liked to keep you in her arms. You felt completely safe in her lap, as if you were floating back into the warmth of her womb. There's a silent bond between you both, through which everything is magically transmitted without the need for gestures or words. You didn't need her presence to feel her immense love for you. There was no separation between you and her; you felt everything she felt as if you were the same person. Perhaps she was a very spiritual woman who passed on her deep knowledge to you, a woman you could often find on her yoga mat surrounded by a ring of incense. She often seemed absent, expressionless, as if she was lost in a wonderful world. I've known of instances where a mother has died at a very young age but has remained very present in her child's life, appearing in her child's dreams, imagination and in the stories other people told them about her. It's also not unusual to hear about a mother suffering from alcoholism or depression whose child sought to save her: caring for her, protecting her, nurturing her. In short, they acted as a mother. Other Piscean mothers are bohemian, with an enormous creative sensitivity and an obvious artistic talent. One thing is certain: the women in your lineage have a hefty unconscious influence on you and their voices resonate deeply within you. They are wise, profound, intuitive, healing, maternal women, with great stories and brilliant dreams that you store in your memory.

You have the power to perceive things that most people couldn't see in their wildest imagination. As a child, your favourite refuge was solitude, and you spent many hours in your room painting or playing with your dolls. Who knows how many school classes you missed because your head was in the clouds. You used your imagination to escape to another place, where infinite possibilities came to life. Pisces is a sign that blurs boundaries, which totalises everything, and many of the emotions you experience during the day aren't your own. You possess an innate vulnerability, and you sometimes find life difficult and hard to cope with. When you feel distressed you retreat into your inner world, and you have therefore become highly introverted. It's easy to find yourself isolated, listening to your favourite music and dreaming up idyllic situations. Unconsciously, you escape into your fantasies to escape from the ugly, routine and ordinary. You need magic, ecstasy and stardust. However, you can't avoid your problems forever; at some point you'll realize that you need to stop procrastinating and face the situation head on. You can't stand conflict and confrontation and, if your partner has their Moon in Scorpio or Aries, your extreme sensitivity will cause you to suffer.

You're incredibly romantic and dreamy. The issue is that you can be extremely naive and unable to distinguish reality from fiction, as if your perception is shrouded in a thick white fog. You make up your own stories in your head and then suffer from delusions and disappointment. You seek true love; the kind that's only possible in fairy tales. You kiss toads believing they will turn into Prince Charming. You tend to idealize and overlook flaws because you don't want your illusion to crumble. Real love scares you, and you end up not getting involved too deeply because you don't want to wake from the dream and ruin the magic. The role of the fragile, lost princess who needs to be rescued is a tempting one. Alternatively, maybe you're the saviour and mother figure who unconditionally throws herself at guys who have serious issues or addictions. One of your problems is that you tend to be nostalgic, and often feel the need to reminisce about wonderful feelings from the past. You can have a passionate romance that lasts just a few days and remember it as the most amazing time of your life.

You possess a highly developed intuition, a keen third eye that can see beyond appearances. If you fearlessly open yourself to this power, you'll no longer be trapped by misleading situations. Moreover, the fact that you easily absorb collective trends gives you a great advantage, since you can touch people's souls through your artistic creations. Another one of your talents is that you can empathize with the pain, misery and suffering of others, because you know how to keep people company in silence. If you're not careful, this Moon sign can lead you to become addicted to certain substances, complex relationships, depressive states, delusions or emotional dependency. Your goal is to mature, ground yourself, feel your body, stay present, be more aware, delve into the truth of reality and stop running away from situations.

ⓘ THIS IS ALSO FOR YOU IF YOU HAVE THE MOON IN THE 12TH HOUSE OR IN CONJUNCTION, OPPOSITION OR SQUARE ASPECT WITH NEPTUNE. EQUALLY, THIS IS FOR YOU IF YOU HAVE NEPTUNE OR PISCES IN THE 4TH HOUSE.

CHAPTER 3

Saturn in relationships

The goal

ħ

SATURN IN RELATIONSHIPS

"I love myself." The quietest. simplest. most powerful. revolution. ever.

NAYYIRAH WAHEED

Saturn is the farthest planet from the Sun that we can observe with the human eye. In ancient times – before the discovery of the spiritual planets Uranus, Neptune and Pluto – it was considered the last planet in the solar system. It's the guardian of the boundary between the personal and the transpersonal, between our human dimension and the divine within us. It teaches us the lessons we need to learn before we can move on to the next level of spiritual growth and, like a strict father, it punishes us if we attempt to take any shortcuts and go beyond what's rightfully ours. To fly high, our roots need to be firmly planted in the ground, otherwise we won't get very far. This strict master is always testing us, examining us to see if we're really ready to break our invisible chains and conquer our dreams. Saturn is the closed door we encounter on our journey, but it's also the key. It confronts us with our limits so that we can overcome them with perseverance, effort and dedication. Our cosmic father tells us, "what we can be, we must be." He tells us that we're immeasurably powerful and pushes us to work on ourselves so that we can understand ourselves. This way, we can surpass ourselves and choose a path of integrity that will lead us to self-realization. Saturn teaches us the value of discipline and effort, and knows how to reward us when we do our very best. We may be artistically gifted, but that won't do us much good if we don't learn the techniques, perfect and master our art and look for a place to exhibit it and attract buyers.

In traditional astrology, Saturn had a terrible reputation. This planet was considered the lord of karma and had a host of problems attributed to it, from obstacles and delays to the most painful limitations. Fortunately, this deterministic view has since changed and we know that what this planet represents is quite different. When this grumpy old man manifests himself, it feels as if life isn't on our side, that we can't move forward how we'd like to, and these situations either bring out the worst in us or the best in us. That's what free will is all about: we can't avoid its lessons, but we can control how we handle what's thrown at us. Ultimately, Saturn wants us to grow up, take responsibility for our lives and stop blaming bad luck and fate for everything that happens to us. He reminds us that we're not the only ones in this world and that the things we do have an impact not only on us but on others. Saturn is the voice of conscience, that inner Jiminy Cricket who helps us distinguish right from wrong and shows us the consequences of our actions from a very early age.

The old master teaches us the limits we have to adhere to in order to operate in this physical dimension. He tells us that there are laws in nature that are absolute and we can't change, such as the law of gravity. We know that we can't do whatever we want in a chaotic way; in this world, there are rules we've set that allow us to coexist and live together in society. If we exceed the speed limit on the road, we can easily be landed with a speeding fine. However, the hardest lesson we have to face is the inevitable passage of time, which causes us to age and lose vitality, but also to achieve greater maturity and wisdom. This planet shows us the ugly face of the world, the harsh reality without any frills, even if we don't like it and want to look the other way. That's why its energy often makes us uncomfortable. We love to lose ourselves in fantasies and illusions, and we often prefer to keep our eyes blindfolded.

When Saturn is linked to love, the goal is to focus on emotional mastery and maturity within relationships. Love isn't something unrealistic or fleeting... it's the result of learning. The old master asks that we learn to love just as we would learn any other art. He asks us to understand that love is respect and admiration, the responsibility of growing and flourishing together. Love includes searching for our loved one's happiness, which is based on our own ability to love. If we don't love ourselves, how can we properly love another?

To have a successful relationship, it's important to make an effort to actively develop our individual potential. The goal is to evolve as free and independent beings, finding happiness in solitude and then sharing it with another human being. Saturn's trials will be arduous and difficult, and we'll experience fear and insecurity. But through the disappointments and frustrations, we'll be given the opportunity to acquire the wisdom necessary to establish a deep, honest and conscious relationship, free from romantic idealizations. The following aspects need to be taken into account:

★ Venus and the Moon in Capricorn or in the 10th house.

★ Venus in conjunction, square aspect or opposition with Saturn. These are aspects of tension and are depicted by a red line on your birth chart.

★ Saturn in the 4th, 7th and 8th house.

THE WISE OLD SORCERESS

Saturn can be related to the feminine archetype that we hold deep within us: the wise old sorceress who hides in solitude in the depths of the forest, the one we can turn to for advice when we're at one of life's crossroads. She knows how to guide those who are lost, because she's accumulated wisdom over time and through experience. This old woman knows how to distinguish the essential from the superficial, the permanent from the transitory. She doesn't lose herself in fantasies that cloud her mind; she knows how to face reality with her eyes wide open. Mature women are undervalued in our society; it seems that a woman who grows old is no longer good for anything. However, in ancient cultures the old women of the tribe had power and dignity; they were the ones who initiated other women, guiding them through their journey to personal maturity. They knew how to connect with mother earth and all life and were an inexhaustible source of knowledge. These women were well aware of the reality of impermanence and understood that the most important quality to cultivate wasn't external beauty, but the light that shone within. They were great storytellers and always gave good advice. They didn't need to aspire to anything, because they knew that they were already everything.

Awakening this feminine archetype is something we should all aim for, and with the passing of the years, we can feel this wise sorceress stirring within us. In relationships, when we leave our childish defence mechanisms behind and mature, we let her in. If we pretend to stay naive and innocent in love, waiting to be rescued from our tower without taking control of our lives, we will suffer. With age, we lose our fear and gain integrity and freedom. We no longer care so much about what people think and we let go of a lot of our shame. We're authentic at all times and we're not afraid to express what we think and feel. We let go of the strict judgements and restrictive standards we unwittingly set ourselves. We no longer struggle to set healthy boundaries because we love ourselves unconditionally. We know how to enjoy life with awareness, respecting all beings and honouring our bodies. We're drawn to work on the necessary healing that will help us become the wise grandmother, to leave a seed of awareness so that future generations will understand the true meaning of the word *love*.

THE SCARS OF SATURN

As children, it's likely that we weren't given a sense of unconditional acceptance, that we weren't taught that we're valuable for who we are and not for what we do. We often felt Saturn's presence when we were reprimanded and punished or prevented from experiencing the world in our own way. We were brought up with a strong sense of duty and obligation, and were criticized when we didn't do things right, and this made us deeply insecure. We felt that we received more love and acceptance from our parents when we did what was right and what was expected of us. To keep people happy, we were constantly on our best behaviour, becoming "model children". We got used to following rules, and little by little we forgot that we had our own power. Without realizing it, our inner universe was reduced to predictable and unspontaneous behaviours, which even today prevent our own light from shining. You probably lacked support and affection from your father, and were very rarely told "well done, daughter, you're doing brilliantly!" Parents are often overwhelmed by the experience of having children and, although their love is unconditional, when they're stressed, they often give the impression that children are more of a burden than a source of happiness. Most of the time they're unable to take care of their sons or daughters because they need to work, and consequently the children are left in the care of others. Even though they were wonderful parents, they may have passed many of their fears on to us. These early relationships with the world are what shape your view of reality and your internal self-image. If those attachments were sometimes a source of disappointment, you may feel deep within yourself that you're not worthy of love, that you're not enough and don't deserve to be loved as you are. This lack of self-esteem is exactly what Saturn asks you to work on, because it can help you let go of your inhibitions and open up to love naturally.

Fear of rejection and abandonment

These early life experiences leave a mark on you, and you can be left fearful of judgement and rejection, especially when it comes to love. You have a tendency to be more controlled and cautious in the way you relate to others. This can lead to extreme shyness, embarrassment or lack of spontaneity when seducing the person you like. You may also find it difficult to express your feelings and ask for what you need from the relationship for fear that these requests won't be well received and you'll get "no" for an answer. The more insecure you feel, the more you close yourself off and the bigger the wall you put up. You may unconsciously come across like an iceberg – cold and distant – when inside you're on fire. You've probably experienced rejection, moments when you've opened yourself up to getting to know someone who seemed interested, but were met only with coldness and indifference. It's not unusual to suffer from the consequences of unrequited love and feel as though you're not worthy of the love that other women seem to get with relative ease. Saturn leads into sadness, deprivation and loneliness again and again. But what it wants is for you to face your fears and insecurities and become an expert in the field of personal relationships. You can't achieve this by hiding from the person you like and waiting for them to make the first move, or by avoiding exposure and vulnerability. If you don't send out a signal that you're interested and risk feeling the dreaded chill of rejection, you'll get old waiting. If that person doesn't want anything to do with you – fine. At least you know and won't waste your time. If you don't open up, you'll never find out how the story ends. It might feel like skydiving for the first time, full of panic and adrenaline, but it's so satisfying when you reach the ground and you've made it. Don't forget to applaud and reward yourself every time you take a step forward and overcome a boundary – you deserve it.

Many women might turn away from the possibility of falling in love out of fear and end up living a solitary existence, absorbed in their work and filling their schedule with goals and routines. Not having time for a relationship is the perfect excuse for not facing their limits, but no matter how satisfying their profession might be, even if it leads to the sweet taste of success, they'll always be left with the bitter feeling that something's missing. Even if they seem completely self-sufficient, deep down they ardently desire to experience romance and be loved intensely. We might think our walls protect us, but in reality they isolate us and prevent us from being happy. In order to love, you need to open your heart and make space in your life so that gap can be filled.

Love and demands

With Saturn, happiness eludes us in various ways, and we always feel somewhat dissatisfied or that we lack affection, even if we have a suitable partner. How often do we start a relationship that seems promising and exciting, only for it to become boring and routine over time? Once the relationship is established, instead of making an effort to keep the spark alive and keep things interesting, we stagnate and settle into dissatisfaction. Alternatively, perhaps we want a person who's daring, adventurous and fun, but we always attract people who are older and too serious. Unconsciously, we're looking for someone who doesn't give us too many headaches, someone who doesn't feel like too much of a risk, even if the relationship lacks magic. We're often our own worst enemy and try to sabotage the good things that happen to us. You might have an incredible relationship with a wonderful person who loves you, and yet you still feel that inner rumbling of mistrust and constant suspicion, always expecting the worst. This is the pessimistic attitude of someone who's always sceptical and expects to be betrayed. People with this attitude interpret everything negatively and believe that the love is fading and not flowing as naturally as it used to. They tend to see their partner's faults and defects, minimize their virtues and be overly critical. Your partner might be madly in love with you and always be there for you, but you frequently find fault and don't value them. Focusing on what's lacking instead of the good things isn't the smartest thing you can do in a relationship, because it's possible that one day your partner will tire of the criticism and leave in search of a warmer, easier place. This goes both ways: you might find yourself in a relationship with someone cold and demanding who always finds ways to limit and criticize your spontaneous behaviour. This person might be austere and boring, and they probably have a negative, distrustful attitude to life, often finding to complain about. You might find yourself in a committed relationship with someone like this, giving them your all and yet still suffering because you feel as though nothing you do is good enough for them. A similar thing happens when you're with someone who's so focused on their professional ambitions that you can never be anything more than second best. As you can see, there are many ways this type of relationship can materialize, but each one leads to frustration.

For Saturn, love is demanding and the ideal man must fulfil at least a two-page list of requirements (and that list is double-sided!) The goal is the ultimate perfect relationship, even if it takes a lifetime to find. Since there's no such thing as perfection and that bar is unattainable, frustration will take hold when this isn't achieved. Even so, people look forward to the future, hoping that, one day, things will change, and the right person will come along. However, it isn't good to judge potential partners too harshly and close the door on people who could offer a lot of positive things for trivial reasons. You might find you get stuck in the pessimistic mindset of "better alone than in bad company". Wanting the best for yourself isn't a bad thing, the problem comes when you treat people like throwaway objects without delving into what really matters, without looking beyond appearances. We can keep our expectations high, but how many of these will actually be reached? And are we capable of giving the same things we expect from others?

We can also become desperate if we've been single for a long time, grabbing the first guy who comes along. One day, your friend introduces you to her new boyfriend and you can immediately see that there's absolutely no connection between them. In fact, they wouldn't stick together with the best glue on the market. It makes you wonder if grasping at straws to avoid being alone really is the best solution. Joking aside, we women are under a lot of pressure to find a steady partner, especially from the age of thirty onwards – our infamous biological clock is ticking, after all. Until that age, you're having fun and enjoying life, and you're told that "you're doing well, just have fun while you still can!" However, as we move into our thirties, the comments start to change. "Maybe your expectations are too high?", "I don't understand how you're still single, you're so cute!" There's a major social stigma surrounding single women, due in part to these messages that we find everywhere: if we don't have a house, a husband, a baby and a stable job, we look incomplete, like we're still figuring our lives out. The anxiety this causes can lead to desperation and believe me, being desperate to find a partner is exactly how not to find one. Being single can be a very positive thing. Use the opportunity to go in search of life, not love. You'll discover that life has a funny way of finding the love you are looking for.

As you can see, Saturn asks us to find balance: we can't be too demanding and set requirements that are impossible for most mortals to meet, nor can we settle for someone who doesn't completely satisfy us just so we're not alone. We need to know how to choose and wait for the person we feel can bring positive things into our lives. In order to choose wisely, we need to be at a time in our lives when we know exactly who we are and what we want from life. Saturn is concerned with what others think and what's "politically correct", and has an unwavering loyalty to the structures that offer us security. Forcing a relationship is a thing of the past; "till death do us part" is a phrase from another era and we no longer have to endure a lifetime of hardship in order to have a lasting relationship. However, many couples today are still held together by constraints such as children, other people's opinions, cultural or religious tradition or various economic reasons. In my opinion, a woman who sacrifices her dreams and happiness for a marriage in exchange for material security is paying too high a price. You spend more energy and life by holding on to a dead relationship than you do by letting go and enjoying a vibrant freedom.

Harsh reality

When Saturn influences our relationships, we're met with the painful reality that our romantic desires and our destiny are two very different paths. I met a girl during a consultation who was having a hard time following a difficult break-up with a co-worker who was also in another relationship. Sometimes you meet someone and get carried away by the things you feel, without considering the consequences. This girl started an on-off relationship with her colleague, and it was filled with false promises that kept her hanging on. Things gradually started to change over time, and he started being more distant and stopped seeking her out like he used to. In response, she tried to get closer to him, but every time she did, she was met with rejection. Eventually, she accepted reality. She wanted to be loved so badly that she didn't stop to really look at the man she was having an affair with and consider whether he was good for her. Soon enough, this man got tired of her complaints and lost sexual interest in her, ditching her and quietly moving on with his relationship. She was left with a lump in her throat, utterly devastated, wondering whether she should quit her job because she never wanted to see him again. Worst of all, she still hoped that he'd regret his decision. Saturn represents harsh reality, the kind that throws cold water over us to wake us from our romantic daydreams. This planet asks us to grow up, to take control of what we want and not accept anything that isn't worthwhile. To take responsibility is to recognize our share of the blame. If this woman had correctly assessed the man in front of her and thought about what he was genuinely offering her, she would have saved herself months of suffering. Saturn shows us the truth of reality and helps us see the things we're not considering. It's ruthless when we try to satisfy our personal desires without considering other people, or when we look the other way and ignore what's really going on as we follow a path that's not our own. There's no point getting involved with someone who's no good for us and who prevents us from growing. We can cry and complain all we want, but we'll end up accepting that our cosmic father is wiser and knows what's really right for us. Contrary to popular belief, Saturn's transits are very positive, because they help us to set boundaries and separate ourselves from toxic people and delusional relationships. They give us the necessary composure to objectively and clearly evaluate what's happening, and not to tolerate abuse or allow anyone to undervalue us.

BEAUTY AND PLEASURE

Family, social and cultural conditioning has shaped our values, and has had a decisive influence on our expectations of and experiences in relationships.

When Saturn is in conjunction with Venus, it inhibits and limits the free expression of sensuality, seduction and beauty – qualities which are inherent to the planet of love. It's quite possible that in childhood, too much emphasis was placed on certain standards of what a woman should be (valuing modesty, etiquette and exemplary "good girl" behaviour) and that sensual, brazen or flashy women who enjoyed their bodies freely were openly rejected. The message taught here was that physical appearance wasn't important and that taking care of your appearance was a symptom of vanity. Perhaps you weren't considered attractive and – out of pure love – were told that outer beauty wasn't the be all and end all, and other qualities such as intelligence, spiritual development and hard work were more important. When a woman is brought up in an environment that represses or rejects sexuality, she's likely to be powerfully conditioned in a way that leads her to inhibit her interest in sex. She may see herself as perverse and feel guilty for being attractive, seductive and having intense sexual desires. On top of society's view of what makes a "good" or "bad" woman, we also have to submit to beauty standards that vary over time. Fashion magazines bombard the public with feminine figures, idealized bodies and faces and unattainable standards, giving women a deep-rooted inferiority complex. There's a reason why cosmetic clinics have spread like wildfire: they offer a "cure" that can help us get what we lack and adjust our bodies to meet these norms. Women ask too much of themselves, and it seems that if we want to be successful with men, we have to embody these stereotypical ideals.

With Saturn in your life, you can look like a beauty queen yet always see the glass as half empty and never quite trust yourself. Often, you don't feel beautiful, and you can't see that special something about you that others might find attractive. You don't think you're valuable, beautiful or worthy of love. However, you also have a deep need to be loved, desired and admired, so a lot of sadness and frustration can build up in you. Sometimes, this lack of self-esteem and self-worth can cause you to neglect your image and look unkempt, as if you don't care about anything. On the contrary, it might also make you very demanding with your physical appearance, constantly touching up your make-up and getting dressed up to the nines in the hope that feel like your beauty will be noticed. We wear false masks in order to seduce, attract and be accepted. That doesn't mean that we can't dress up and make ourselves feel beautiful – because taking care of ourselves inside and out *is* an act of self-love. The image we reveal to the world says a lot about us and reflects how we feel, and speaks of our self-esteem and lifestyle. However, it's something that should come from deep within, not from seeking external validation. It seems that as we get older, these things become less important, and we feel more comfortable in our skin and more self-confident. Time puts everything into perspective and helps us understand that we can offer so much more than an image that will wither away sooner or later.

WHEN WILL THE FUN START?

Saturn limits the free expression of the goddess of love and teaches her that she can enjoy herself, but with good measure and responsibility. Pleasure is strongly conditioned by security, rules and restrictions. I see a lot of Saturn in those women who are too serious and structured, who find it difficult to indulge themselves and enjoy life. They might see a beautiful dress in a shop window, but under no circumstances will they buy it. They don't do crazy things, always prioritizing what's right and what's appropriate in every situation. They're too cautious and controlled and never reach beyond the limits they've set for themselves without realizing it. They often judge people harshly if they don't fit the mould and the labels they've created. This isn't to say that you're like that, but if you take a moment to carefully reflect on your life, at some point you've likely deprived yourself of fun and admired other women who weren't afraid to let their hair down. How many times have we wondered if sleeping with a guy was the right thing to do, even though, deep down, we really wanted to? "I really want to have sex with him, but we've only been on three dates, what will he think of me?" If we do it too soon, we'll be judged as "easy" and placed in the "unsuitable for a serious relationship" category. But there's no set rule: you can have sex on the first date and end up marrying the guy, or wait three weeks before sleeping together and he still might ghost you afterwards. With Saturn, it can take us a while to feel confident enough to be intimate. We don't open up right away, we're fearful of sexuality, of becoming one with the other person, of revealing our deepest emotions. Essentially, it's about breaking down those barriers and starting to experience the beautiful sensation of doing what we feel like doing and what makes us feel good. Life is passing us by and we can't afford to miss opportunities to have fun and be happy. How often have we heard people say, "When I retire, I'll go on that trip" or "I'll be happy when I'm in a relationship." Our hopes and dreams are always projected onto a hypothetical future. We set ourselves so many limits and obstacles without realizing the power we have. Too often we've been told what we can and can't do, and we've been frightened into believing that what we want is crazy. Dull people specialize in demotivating dreamers and dimming our bright ideas. Of course, not everything is possible, and Saturn forces us to assess the feasibility of what we want. However, it also tells us that if we try hard and do our best, we can find the right path for us. The problem is that we mistranslate its message, and fear often trumps desire. Just know that when someone tells you something's impossible, they're talking about their own limitations, not yours. The answer to everything is NOW. When else? If an opportunity to savour life, get what you deserve and have fun presents itself, don't hesitate and go for it. Don't take life so seriously, let go of control and have fun; you deserve to be happy.

OVERCOMING FEAR

Behind all these difficult experiences is the fear that paralyzes us. We fear that our partner will stop loving us and leave us. We fear that we'll be rejected, that things will change, that we'll be alone, that we'll suffer... We try to fit in, protecting ourselves with a list of requirements. We strive to be liked, to do things well and obtain the recognition we never had as children. We give our all and make an effort;

we do our duty and often don't get much in return. Saturn tells us to give just the right amount in our relationships – no more, no less – so as not to neglect the development of other parts of life that make us feel fulfilled. It's important to start overcoming these fears and escape this conditioning, transforming the strict standards we've created and all the rules that govern our behaviour. We need to free ourselves from unconscious slavery bit by bit, to leave our comfort zone, break with rigidity and find fluidity. We need to love ourselves deeply and express who we are and what we feel with courage and honesty. We need to understand that the person we love will disappoint us to some extent, just as we will disappoint them, but we shouldn't try to correct or change them, nor should we allow them to do the same with us. The key is to fill ourselves with gratitude for all the good things we have right now, rather than complaining and focusing on the things we lack. When we're full, we don't need anyone. This is exactly what Saturn asks us to do: to need each other less and to be together because our shared moments fill us with joy; to find the courage to follow our heart with responsibility and maturity, and without fearing pain. As the great Chavela Vargas said, "Love without measure, without limit, without complex, without permission, without courage, without advice, without doubt, without price, without cure, without anything. Do not be afraid to love, you will shed tears with love or without it."

CHAPTER 4

Uranus in relationships

A free spirit

⛢

URANUS IN RELATIONSHIPS

I refuse to live in the ordinary world as ordinary women. To enter ordinary relationships. I want ecstasy. I am a neurotic – in the sense that I live in my world. I will not adjust myself to the world. I am adjusted to myself.

ANAÏS NIN

Uranus represents the freedom and change provided by the universe. Its name means "star-crowned sky", symbolizing that open, endless space that holds infinite possibilities. It's the energy that encourages us to free ourselves from stagnation in the most creative ways. We all want to be free, to change our reality and do new and exciting things that help us escape boredom and routine. However, when the universe turns our lives upside down, we don't understand what it's trying to tell us and panic because we don't feel ready. We'd rather remain in our comfort zone, where we're comfy and content – even if we're bored out of our minds. However painful, frustrating and uncomfortable our existence may be, we cling to it because it's what we know, rather than opening ourselves up to something completely new. Uranus shakes our lives up like a cocktail shaker and gets us to switch things around. It frees us from restrictions and limitations, from routines that no longer inspire us, from formalities and social conventions that are outdated and obsolete. It tells us that there's something better waiting for us, that a new world could take shape right before our eyes if we dare to leap into the unknown. We know that life doesn't follow a logical order. Our plans don't always go as we expect and there are events that we can't foresee or control. When Uranus is present, we often get this feeling of risk, uncertainty and fear of the future because we've already experienced many unforeseen situations that have upset us emotionally in the past. This planet manifesting in our lives is scary because deep down we don't like change. However, we must understand that crises are magical moments that break down the illusions we try to convince ourselves are real. We need to rewrite the script and create a new life story, and this time we can forge the free, luminous life we desire. Uranus tells us that in order to change everything we must take risks, be willing to experience the discomfort of transition and accept nothing less than the love and full alignment we deserve. Even if the destination is unclear, we must trust the journey.

Uranus wants us to express our unique, original and different side, even if that means we don't fit in with anyone else. We're all special and have our own unique qualities, ones that are ours and ours alone. Every one of us, without exception, is born with something new and beautiful that we can offer the world to make life richer. No one enters into this life without any genuine talent or potential. Why do we strive to be like everyone else? Why do we compare ourselves with others? We tend to set aside our fullest potential in order to fit in with the opinion of the masses. All too often, we lessen ourselves so that others don't feel insecure. It's normal to want to belong to a group; no one wants to feel like the odd one out or be rejected by others. However, when we seek acceptance in this world, we're turning our back on Uranus. Its vibration inspires us to do things our own way and be true to our authentic selves, transcending roles and standards that no longer represent us. It's important to have the courage to follow your own path and find your own voice, even if it goes against what others think.

THE URANIAN CONNECTIONS

In our relationships, Uranus encourages us to be free and break away from any restrictions imposed by family, religion, beliefs or society. It doesn't want us to be defined by anything or to be pigeonholed into rigid standards without first exploring different positions. We've been told that the best way to love is within a traditional couple, but Uranus affirms that we can be more creative and explore other options that respect our personal freedom. We'll have phases when we need to break the rules, take risks and try new things, and other times when we'll hold on tightly to stability. Fate and the events it imposes will bring about change for us. We all oscillate between the need to find a life partner, make a home and put down roots and the desire for variety, fun and exciting experiences. Venus and the Moon want togetherness, closeness and belonging. Uranus wants us to make space to fulfil ourselves. If we become attached to someone and lose ourselves, we can no longer be creative. There's a real inner battle between the desire to have a deep, committed relationship and the need to maintain our space. At times, we'll be looking for a serious and stable relationship, and at other times we'll prioritize being by ourselves without making a definite commitment to anyone. In a Uranian couple, it's common for one partner to express a need for more autonomy and the other partner to be more interested in seeking intimacy and closeness. These two positions can even alternate between the two partners over time. Reconciling both tendencies will be a lifelong challenge, but no one ever said it would be easy. The main aspects to consider in order to know whether Uranus will provide an intense challenge for us when it comes to relationships are the following:

★ Venus or the Moon in conjunction, opposition or square aspect with Uranus. These are aspects of tension and are depicted with a red line in your birth chart.
★ Uranus in the 1st, 4th or 7th house.
★ Venus or the Moon in Aquarius or in the 11th house.

REBEL HEART

Uranus is the revolution we need to move things forward. We're attuned to its energy when we dare to go against the grain and think for ourselves. I see a lot of Uranus in those women who were bold enough to go beyond what was deemed appropriate, who didn't want to follow traditions, disobeyed the norms of their community and fought for their rights. They were sources of inspiration, true revolutionaries, because they dared to explore different possibilities and broke away from the standards of their time. As a result, they were stigmatized, shunned, accused or locked up for being crazy. If we go back to even darker times, thousands of women were accused of witchcraft and killed – especially those who listened to their intuition, connected with the cycles of the universe and prepared herbal remedies that healed illnesses and ailments. They possessed knowledge that they inherited from their ancestors. We know that many ancient cultures had a rich history of magic, folklore and mythology, and they knew how to listen to the Earth's wisdom. These women probably performed magical rituals, connected with their bodies and enjoyed their sexuality. They were truly anti-establishment, and for this they were tortured and burned.

We are the result of all of these women, who endured centuries of assaults and trauma so that we could enjoy the light of liberty. For every vibrant freedom we've achieved, hundreds of hard battles were fought in the darkness. We collectively remember these wounds, and many women are afraid to explore different options, speak out for new ideas and engage in things that aren't so socially accepted. When I was a child, my mother was involved in alternative therapies, and I remember hearing the word "witch" more than once. It was used in a humorous way, but it hid contempt that made me feel disgusted and rejected, as if it opened a deep wound inside me. Fortunately, things are changing and we're regaining our power. By recovering this ancient knowledge, we're becoming aware of our capacity to heal ourselves and awakening our interest in developing our potential and creating the life we desire.

DON'T BE LIKE EVERYONE ELSE

Just like those fantastic women, if Uranus is prominent in your make-up, you are and have always felt *different*. You can try to hide it and wear a mask to fit in, but there will always be a part of you that doesn't deeply connect with others. There's an uncomfortable difference between you and others and even in company, you often feel alone. You've never felt that sense of belonging, like you're a part of the group. Even if you try to integrate, you'll often feel awkward. You feel as though no one can understand you or put themselves in your shoes, and you may hide parts of yourself because you think you don't fit in with anyone else. You might have experienced needing comfort and emotional support and being met only with indifference. It's not unusual for you to have occasionally experienced rejection from others, and you're still afraid of it happening again.

To avoid these uncomfortable feelings, you can become a true rebel without a cause, disobeying the rules and smashing through any restrictions imposed on you – an indomitable soul looking for freedom and the ability to go wherever the wind takes her. You don't adapt to society and flee from the slightest hint of control. You're a non-conformist who doesn't tolerate labels or limitations. Alternatively, you may go the other way, becoming obedient, compliant and conventional as a way of seeking acceptance. You cling to the familiar, shying away from anything new and prioritizing stability. If you take the latter path, you'll probably end up in a serious, committed relationship, though you'll eventually discover that you feel as lonely and empty as you would be on your own. When you become overly attached to your partner and turn your back on the unique, free part of yourself, Uranus will burst into your life – and it's not unusual for you to escape out of the nearest window, find a lover or travel to a distant island in the Pacific.

You're sure to experience more than one unexpected break-up, and you'll be left stunned and unable to understand what's happened or how to react. You need love and emotional support, yet life gives you rejection, break-ups and unexpected events, one after the other. It's possible that you attract detached, unpredictable types who aren't looking for emotional commitment; people who come and go, and don't attach themselves definitively. You'll be left frustrated because you want something stable and permanent, but you always seem to meet the stereotypical wild, rebellious and emotionally unattached guy.

In a recent consultation, an upset woman was telling me that she'd recently experienced a very traumatic break-up. She'd met a girl a few months ago, and things started out well. She was really into her, and the romance was intense and passionate. The relationship was moving fast and they'd made lots of future plans – they had even been on holiday together. However, the girl slowly started distancing herself, becoming practically unavailable. One day, she unexpectedly broke off the relationship, leaving the woman feeling totally dejected. It seems that Uranus has a bit of a temper – every time you're feel great and throw yourself into a promising relationship, you're forced to let go. But this planet intervenes when you betray yourself and over-adapt to a relationship, pouring all your energy into it as if that person is the solution to all your problems. It intervenes when you lose too much of your self-identity to truly belong with your partner. If your whole world revolves around that person and you've stopped doing what you love, don't be surprised if complications soon arise.

We sustain relationships that really should be over and have long since lost their magic simply because we don't like the idea of being alone again. You can adapt to the old conventions within a relationship, you can even plan a dream wedding in preparation for your happily ever after, but unless you somehow include Uranus' energy within your life and your relationship, tragedy is around the corner. Your life plan can't revolve around one person, because there's absolutely no guarantee that this person will stay by your side.

Some Uranian women may stay in restrictive relationships with partners who don't consider their wants and needs or let them have any fun in their lives. They remain by their partner's side physically, but their hearts are frozen solid, as if a part of them has long since left. Some endings seem to be written in the stars, yet somehow they never quite materialize and instead the relationship drags on forever, preventing new, bright beginnings. At first, break-ups are painful, but eventually you'll discover that the change was a breath of fresh air that helped you escape monumental boredom. If you lose someone, but end up finding yourself, then you've certainly won.

The main problem is that we tend to overlook Uranus, as if it doesn't belong to us. Then it appears all of a sudden, disrupting our life and showing us that we can't deny it forever. What's clear is that you're sidelining an important part of yourself, one that needs freedom and room to breathe within the partnership. Then, it's often the other person or the circumstances themselves that change to create that space. When we're unaware of our inner contradictions, and only take Venus and the Moon into account, fate brings Uranus into our lives, opening our eyes to a new reality and forcing us to explore dimensions beyond ourselves. The planet encourages us to seek a relationship that's not based on finding security or filling our emptiness. Love doesn't have to conform to socially accepted patterns; it has to vibrate with what our hearts desire, even if it's out of the norm or even scandalous. We may be liberal and open-minded now but not so long ago, same-sex relationships were considered a crime and punished. Even now, we're still shocked when a mature woman falls in love and walks hand in hand with a much younger guy. In my consultations, I've met women who find it difficult to openly express that they're in a same-sex relationship, as if it's something they need to whisper. Many people still believe that if an adult woman decides to be single, or doesn't want to have children, she's strange or emotionally disturbed. If Uranus is heavily associated with your love life and you're of a certain age, it's not uncommon for your relationships to have been a little unusual, to say the least.

Embracing Uranus means daring to be yourself and respecting your true essence. If you do, you'll probably become the odd one out in the family; the black sheep who doesn't conform to the rules and behaves eccentrically. You'll most likely be criticized, and the dull people in this world will be angry with you for letting your own light shine. You'll need to leave many friends and relationships behind. There will come a time when you won't care what people say, because you'll know that being alone by choice is the price of true freedom. You know how to be alone and you passionately surrender yourself to life, expanding your boundaries, awakening an artistic or humanitarian vision and doing the things that make you happy. Suddenly you find yourself deeply loving your uniqueness, and you value and accept yourself as you are. Unlike other people, your light shines brighter every day, instead of gradually fading away. One day, without knowing how or why, you'll find yourself next to someone wonderful who truly loves you, and you'll fall head over heels for them. Best of all, this person loves all those unique, strange and eccentric parts of you, the parts that are undoubtedly the most beautiful. This is a love that lets you be you, that respects your space and freedom and sweetly accompanies you on life's journey.

FEAR OF COMMITMENT

The classic fear of commitment that often occurs in these scenarios stems from a deep fear of rejection and abandonment. We don't want to get hurt again and may choose not to commit to anyone in particular. The idea of "better alone than in bad company" might stick with us for a long time, because we don't want to be emotionally upset by anyone. We might be distant, indifferent and unconsciously detached when we meet someone new; it's a form of control and protection. When we sense that a person is getting too close, all our alarm bells go off, and we may unwittingly sabotage the relationship. The more we feel that we might be falling for someone, the more we feel the need to escape. We don't want to re-experience the pain of a break-up, so we avoid real intimacy.

Other times, we may venture out to experience that love, but when it becomes too stable or the next step has to be taken, we're confronted by doubt and insecurity. There's an unconscious fear that something bad might happen when everything's going well, and we feel deeply anxious that the relationship will end abruptly. Boycotting, running away, escaping and being hot and cold ensues, because we unconsciously associate a serious relationship with feeling overwhelmed, losing our freedom and suffering. We may even find a promising relationship boring and find ourselves dedicated to the idea of uncommitted relationships that we consider exciting, even though they don't deeply satisfy us. One thing is clear, if Uranus is very present in your life, your love for a person increases when they're able to give you the breathing space you need. On the other hand, if they try to limit and restrict you, or become too demanding, you'll soon become overwhelmed. You don't like routine and always try to make changes that will add a little oomph to the relationship. You're someone who needs a good dose of sparkle and magic.

UNCONVENTIONAL RELATIONSHIPS

If Uranus is very present in your life, you'll eventually discover that what you need is a relationship free of ties and obligations. You want to be with someone because you both want to be together, not because you've been forced to formalize your connection because it's the right thing to do. Having to sign a piece of paper and swear an oath at the altar to secure your commitment and confirm that you'll be together "until death you do part" doesn't really fit with your free and creative side. If you decide it is right for you, you'll probably manage to turn the event into something original and out of the ordinary. You'll likely find being with your partner twenty-four hours a day suffocating, and you won't want to keep them up to date on your every move. Almost without trying, you can form romantic connections that are different, eccentric and transgressive, because part of you has a deep need for adrenaline and fun. It's not unusual for you to be in a long-distance relationship or with someone who's away periodically for work.

You've probably tried some out-of-the-box experiences and ventured into unconventional relationships at some stage in your life. Traditional monogamy is sold as the main option, and generally we prefer it, with many people in very happy long-term partnerships. However, with the powerful Uranus at work, for some this might be a choice made as a result of strong social conditioning, even if they don't initially recognize it. Wanting to stay with a person forever and giving them emotional loyalty and sexual exclusivity can be wearing, and it can generate a lot of dissatisfaction over time. There's a part of us that longs to find our "better half", that special person we can share values and put down roots with. We believe that our soulmate is out there somewhere. They'll fit us like a glove and be able to satisfy all our emotional, romantic, sexual and spiritual needs. An all-in-one so perfect and ideal that we won't need to look for anyone else for the rest of our lives. Compared to those of previous decades, modern romantic demands have increased. These demands are for stability and exclusivity, but also endless mystery, passion and magic... Although that's more wishful thinking than reality.

Due to the unlikelihood of experiencing all this within one traditional relationship, many people who are heavily influenced by Uranus feel attracted to transgressive relationships that break with convention: polyamory, "open" relationships, friends with benefits... Moreover, we're currently living through a time of sexual revolution, and many are daring to explore or at least feel curious about sex that's unconventional and out of the ordinary: threesomes, booty calls, tantric sex, swinging...

If we're honest with ourselves, there's probably been a time or two when we felt attracted to another person while we were in a relationship, and we were tempted to flirt and go along with it. We end up feeling tremendously guilty because we really love the person we're with. So we decide we're not going to act on that feeling at all, instead prioritizing loyalty to our partner. Here, Saturn wins the battle because we don't consider crossing that boundary. But other people simply dare to tell their partner how they're feeling, even if it means losing them. You might think that if you really loved them, you wouldn't feel these things in the first place, but it's not always that simple. There are lifelong relationships where two people might love each other very much, but perhaps the spark of passion has waned too much over the years. One day, one of them experiences an unexplained attraction to another person, and instead of cheating on their partner, they dare to speak honestly about how they're feeling. Hypothetically, if the couple comes to an agreement, they may decide to open the relationship: they give each other permission to have sex outside the relationship without considering it infidelity. These people find that having other sexual partners breaks the monotony of the relationship and makes their sex life with their partner more exciting. We might think that this hides a profound fear of true intimacy and deep emotional commitment, but these people are being honest, vulnerable and committed to their partners, even more so than in many situations where partners cheat because the relationship is long dead, and they only stay together for the children or for financial stability. Polyamory is a step further, opening the possibility of not only having sex with other people, but of falling in love with several of them.

In all these non-normative relationships, we struggle with dramas caused by jealousy. We can question whether we women are really prepared for such relationships because, as I've mentioned elsewhere in this book, it's more difficult for us to separate sex and emotion. It's clear that a degree of emotional detachment is required for this type of relationship, but how can we detach ourselves from intense emotions without disconnecting from them altogether? There are also other energetic structures in our birth chart that strongly condition us and push us in the opposite direction – such as the need for passionate romance. This makes us focus obsessively on the other person, feeling the magic and ecstasy of love. We also develop attachments and need emotional security and belonging. Knowing that this person is there and won't suddenly leave us brings us a sense of peace and tranquillity. This pulls on us a lot, and open relationships seem so far removed from what we really desire from love. On the other hand, it's important to distinguish whether women who experiment with these options do so freely or whether they're forced to do so because it's what their partners want, so they keep them happy so as not to lose them. Or perhaps having more sex and romance is just a phase, or a way of getting a dizzying high and escaping the emptiness we all occasionally feel inside. We want freedom, excitement and fun, but we also want to do the right thing. And this is where the eternal dilemma between Uranus and Saturn comes into play. A non-normative relationship must include the latter, and consensual rules must be established so that no one gets hurt.

Nowadays, we might be more willing to reconcile these strong inner contradictions that we feel, but decades ago Uranus wreaked havoc because we had to obey much stricter social norms. I can give you an example of a real case that perfectly illustrates how Uranus' energy creeps into relationships, even if we don't want it to.

Boy meets girl, and they enjoy a passionate whirlwind romance. After a few months, in the heat of love, she unexpectedly discovers that the man is married and has several children, and is left deeply disappointed. At the time, this was a real scandal within her family, and the blame was placed on the woman, who was deemed a "homewrecker". Her mother, a widow, felt terribly overwhelmed by the situation, so to get her daughter away from this person, she dragged her and her siblings to another city and they started their lives from scratch. These girls probably had a Uranian structure associated with their Moon, because they had to suddenly detach themselves from their whole world to start a new life. However, this move didn't help, nor did it make the protagonist of this story forget about the man because Pluto and Neptune were intensely influencing her way of experiencing this romance. They continued to see each other; he visited her frequently, which resulted in his wife finding out about the affair. His wife had strong, repressed Uranus energy inside her, and when their marriage became too serious and predictable, and all the initial spark was lost without either of them doing anything about it, the planet unexpectedly appeared in the form of his lover. We know that when we cling to strict structures and established relationship norms, the unacknowledged part of the relationship eventually sneaks through the cracks, blowing everything up. However, this woman couldn't get her husband to leave his lover, and instead of breaking off the relationship and being free, she clung to Saturn and kept the relationship going because of the children, the economic stability and what people might say. She also feared being single and breaking the sacred bond of marriage and wanted to do what she thought was right, even at the cost of her own happiness. He was driven by desire and managed to maintain both relationships at the same time (a forced, painful polyamory). Both women shared this man in a structured way: his wife kept him at home on weekdays (I don't know if their marriage was purely for show or whether they continued to have a sexual relationship), and the other woman enjoyed his company on weekends. That's how things stayed practically all their lives. The person who played the role of the "other woman" had to put up with social stigma and rejection. She ended up making a sacrifice for love (Neptune) and because of her difficulty to let go (Pluto). Maybe she should have left that man to avoid suffering, but she eventually discovered that she loved the space it afforded her. She was free to see her friends, to live freely and unattached, and she learned to enjoy her solitude. This intermittent relationship kept the spark more alive, and she ended up adjusting to the unusual situation. Perhaps unconsciously, she began to connect with that hidden Uranian part of herself that needs freedom and breathing space in a relationship. At the same time, she'd found a way to feed her Neptunian idealization for a little longer and continue clinging on to the relationship that her Pluto demanded.

LOVE AND FREEDOM

If you look back on your relationships, you'll find that the more hooked you were and the more you wanted to pursue the person, the more they slipped away from you. Conversely, when you were more laid-back and didn't take things too seriously, the person you were interested in was much more devoted to you. When we fall in love, we often lose our way. The intensity of our emotions takes over and we're afraid to show ourselves as we really are. We don't know how to manage what we feel and hide many aspects of ourselves in order to please the other person. We place too much importance on everything that happens, and we're more concerned with how the relationship is progressing than with having a good time. The moment we embrace our Uranus, we want to get to know the person not only romantically, but as a friend and companion we can trust and truly be ourselves with: no masks, no pretence. You're magic, you don't need games, tricks or strategies to earn their love. You're not a challenge for someone to conquer, nor do you have to be difficult to obtain. You don't have to cancel an exciting date you really want to go on. You have to be you and always do what you feel like doing, without expectations, and without thinking about the consequences. If you're authentic and reveal what makes you unique, you'll exude an incredible, fascinating magnetism.

Another important detail is that you should never, under any circumstances, date someone you need to change, nor should you let anyone else do this to you. Accepting your differences and respecting each other's space is essential if you want to have a healthy relationship. It's vital that you both have hobbies, interests and independent motivations, while also planning different, original and fun things to do together to avoid falling into a boring routine.

A partnership is not a unit, it is two different parts held together by a bond that must be flexible and creative in order for the couple to adapt to each other's emotional fluctuations. You need to learn to live with the idea that the relationship could end at any time because the other has the free will to leave whenever they want. Moreover, a relationship based on freedom features no power games, unreasonable attachments, deceptions or manipulations; there's no need for them. The planet asks for a partnership in which you both walk hand in hand, and neither is better than the other.

CHAPTER 5

Neptune in relationships

The exaltation of love

NEPTUNE IN RELATIONSHIPS

I love you neither with my heart nor with my mind.
My heart might stop, my mind can forget.
I love you with my soul because my soul never stops or forgets.
RUMI

Neptune is a deeply spiritual energy. It symbolizes unconditional love and sensitivity that transcends the individual. Neptune connects us with the yearning for transcendence, to merge with something greater than ourselves and rediscover that we're all one; that there's a sacred consciousness linked to the whole of life in every living being. The planet dissolves the boundaries of the individual self, it knocks down the hard, strict boundaries we erected to avoid feeling our emotions and protect ourselves from pain – the boundaries that separate us from other beings. The Vedas, the ancient sacred texts of India, refer to the term *maya*, meaning "illusion", to express the idea that the world we perceive with the physical senses isn't as solid and real as we think it is; it only shows us part of the truth. What we can observe is a reflection of our inner selves. From the perspective of eternity, we're a drop in the middle of a vast ocean that believes itself to be separate from the rest. Everything alive – trees, birds, stones – vibrates and is part of a universal soul. That great ocean we belong to is a great source of infinite love, a place where there's no pain, no loneliness, no emptiness, no death. Love and hate, order and chaos, good and evil, life and death mean nothing to it; all experiences are one. Past, present and future exist simultaneously, but as humans we can only understand time in a linear way. For Neptune, there's no difference between the self and the exterior, between dreaming and wakefulness, between possible and impossible, between conscious and unconscious...

Neptunian experiences push us down the rabbit hole, where things don't follow a logical order, and everything gets turned on its head. This is why these experiences are notorious for leading us into confusion; when venturing through this plane of reality, certain boundaries are necessary in order for us not to become lost. What is a dream and what is real? By dissolving the rigid edges of the mind, the planet connects us to the mysteries of life that transcend the ordinary: magic, synchronicity, visions, altered states of consciousness, meditation, lucid dreaming, premonition, intuition, the mystical and any experience that can be labelled unbelievable or impossible. As we experience the planet's influence and become receptive to its experience, we become more awake and aware of everything around us.

THE INNER REFUGE

Neptune connects us with the longing to return to the source of infinite love from which we came. When the archetype is very much alive in us, everyday life can become heavy and difficult to bear. The harshness of the world – the suffering, the responsibilities and the problems – can become difficult and often overpowering. Resonant and spiritual people are creatures of two worlds: one part of us lives here, but another part of us wants to escape elsewhere, as if remembering that we don't really belong here. We're extremely receptive and have a gift for noticing the subtle fluctuations of energy and mood in the atmosphere like a kind of psychic sponge. We're simply more sensitive to what other people feel.

A clear example of this resonance is how a mother can sense what's happening to her baby even when she's in another room. Our sensitive antennae leave us too exposed and most of the emotions we experience during the day are not our own. There's so much sensitivity that we often can't distinguish whether an emotion is ours or that of the person next to us. Everything that happens to others affects us as if it were happening to us directly, which is why we have such a deep empathic capacity. This means that most of the time, as a protective mechanism, we close ourselves off from this energy and stop feeling. We keep a very busy schedule and focus on our daily tasks, thus avoiding contact with the things that hurt us deeply. We don't want to know anything about these magical worlds or anything that we can't understand with our rational mind. Another way to escape from such sensitivity is to seek refuge in a magical and beautiful inner world, where there are countless possibilities and wonderful sensations. Our bubble is a safe space, a place of sacred intimacy where we can connect with our dreams, desires and hopes. When Neptune conjuncts Venus and the Moon, a romantic relationship is the perfect refuge to escape to. Our weariness with life is sometimes so unbearable that we use our crusade for love to avoid our existential emptiness. Neptune is the natural ruler of Pisces and rules the 12th house. The main aspects to look at in your birth chart and keep in mind are as follows:

★ Venus or the Moon in conjunction, opposition or square aspect with Neptune. These are aspects of tension and are depicted with a red line in your birth chart.

★ Neptune in the 1st, 4th, 5th or 7th house.

★ Venus or the Moon in Pisces or in the 12th house.

THE YEARNING FOR AN IDYLLIC LOVE

Venus is exceptionally intense in the waters ruled by Neptune.

Like a wild river, the archetype eventually consumes us and the search for love takes on an almost mythological quality. There's an unconscious fascination with experiencing a legendary romance worthy of the most extraordinary fairy tale. Like a princess in a castle, we await the arrival of a charming prince who'll rescue us from our unbearable loneliness. We long to lose ourselves in another person, to experience a meeting of souls, a mystical union, a deep and unforgettable connection. Love loses its ordinary dimension, and we search for that perfect person who understands us without our needing to say a word.

When an encounter is influenced by Venus and Neptune, we experience total ecstasy… A sea of emotions and feelings, which flood us completely and end up clouding our judgement. We project our unconscious desires onto this person and make them the answer to all our romantic needs. We tend to distort the image of the person we're excited by, attributing all the positive qualities we desire to them and ignoring their faults. This happens to most of us when we fall in love: love blinds us and, most of the time, we're left in a haze, overlooking the parts of the relationship that aren't so wonderful. As the relationship becomes less idealized, we begin to spot things that previously went completely unnoticed, and we slowly start to wake up from the dream. In this astral configuration, the situation is very pronounced. This exaltation of romantic love makes us want to live in a dream forever, idealizing the experiences we have and emphasizing how beautiful they make us feel. We might be up to our necks in truly problematic and destructive situations, but we won't take our partner off their pedestal. We find it hard to see the relationship for what it is and ultimately, disappointment and disillusionment follow.

Difficulty establishing genuine love

The routines, responsibilities and problems within a relationship leave no room for a fairy tale. Differences will always arise between two people – after all, they're looking for different things, feel differently and have different emotional needs. In a partnership, communicating and finding common ground is necessary, and this often undermines the initial enchantment. A relationship requires work, effort and dedication. Romantic movies end with a passionate kiss, but they never show how years of living together have worn that love away. With Neptune, there's a lot of fear that the magic will fizzle out, that what we're left with won't be what we dreamed of, that we'll experience the less beautiful parts of the relationship. This can cause us not to pair up with anyone and avoid real love and true intimacy in various ways.

One is to fool around with a lot of people without making a deep commitment to anyone in an attempt to avoid the frustration of disappointment. Another is to search for the perfect person and fall in love with that idea, rather than the person in front of us. We might also be the ones to unconsciously project the image of a beautiful, perfect woman, making the other person fall in love with us without ever showing the less pleasant parts of our personality – that is, we stop being ourselves and become another person's idea of perfection. When our true selves are revealed, the pain of disappointment appears. Our relationships repeatedly leave us with a bitter taste in our mouths as we struggle to understand how something so perfect failed.

NEPTUNIAN RELATIONSHIPS

When romantic love merges with unconditional love, it takes on an elevated dimension, though it comes with a good deal of sacrifice. We want to experience that fusion, that feeling of re-connecting with the whole of creation and feeling completely safe and happy again. We receive so much love from the Divine Source and we want to share it. However, instead of sprinkling it around the world, we concentrate it all on one person who's probably not worthy of such consideration. We run the risk of losing ourselves in this other person and we give up so much for that relationship. We completely lose sight of the bigger picture, sacrifice our own needs, give more love than we receive and, at some point, we may feel used. We're left waiting for a romantic miracle that will give us what we so deeply long for. Neptune leads us into this trap time and time again, and it's normal for the resulting disappointment to be directly proportional to the expectations we placed on an unrealistic relationship. We set up a series of tricks, self-deceptions and justifications to avoid contact with reality. If you catch yourself excusing your partner too many times, believe me, they're not the right person for you. If you have to tell your friends "you just don't get it" more than once, it's best to get out. With Neptune, there'll be no shortage of hidden, deceitful, clandestine, unattainable, confused and utopian romances... There are countless situations that might occur, but broadly speaking they are as follows.

The saviour

With Neptune working behind the scenes, it's not unusual for you to be irresistibly attracted to some troubled, lonely, substance-addicted guy at some point in your life. He likely had a difficult childhood or is unable to face the world and solve his problems. You'll view him as a helpless, lonely, misunderstood child, and you'll feel for him. He'll seem fragile and in need of your love, and you'll want to save him. You only focus on the best parts of him and on your relationship's potential, even if no one else can see it. You feel that you're the only person in the world who understands him, and you wish your love could heal him and rescue him from his unhappiness. You might spend months, even years, deluding yourself, ignoring all your limits and hoping for a happy ending that never comes. But there will come a time when the relationship becomes unsustainable. You'll eventually become worn out from all the disappointments that have accumulated over time and you'll start to see the reality of the situation. The person you had idealized will crumble in front of you and you'll realize how much you sacrificed your happiness for this person. You can't sustain a non-reciprocal relationship with acceptance alone; love is not enough to save anyone from their addictions, traumas and emotional failings. If you dig deeper into what's happened, you'll realize that the one you were really trying to save was yourself. You're the fragile child in need of love who wants to be rescued from her unbearable loneliness. You see, with Neptune everything is intertwined; nothing is as it seems.

Crazy in love

If Neptune is the protagonist in your relationships, you have a tendency to fall madly in love with bohemian, mystical or artistic types, who will bewitch you with their magical sensitivity. You should avoid the temptation to lose yourself in their world and do crazy things. And by crazy, I mean you quitting your job, saying goodbye to your life, packing your bags and going with them when they tell you they're going to live in Bali within two months of meeting you. You never know, it might just work out, they seem perfect for you... You want the same things, and they're charming; a real dream come true. Even though it might sound incredibly romantic, the chances of you falling from cloud nine at the same breakneck speed you flew up there are high. Neptune is like that, an improper romantic, and disappointments in love occur under his influence. Under its effects, it's as if you're on a binge; boundaries are blurred, and your identity is no longer clear. It pushes you to merge with the other person, to lose yourself and absorb their way of seeing life. They drive you so crazy that if they ask you to come with them to the jungle to do drugs, despite the fact that such things terrify you, you go and do it. Or if they suggest you get a tattoo of each other's names after two weeks of knowing each other, before you know it, you're lying in their favourite tattoo artist's studio. When you look back on it, you might smile or you might shake your head… who knows. What is certain though, is that when you think about it, you realize how much you stopped being you and became a "we".

Undefined romances

What are we? Undefined romances are classically Neptune. You're drawn to guys who don't want a commitment like you're a moth to a flame. You get hung up on that relationship for too long, hoping that one day, as if by magic, that man will wake up knowing that you're the woman of his dreams and run off to find you. You forever maintain this illusion and hope and embellish the relationship with countless fantasies, to avoid the truth: he just doesn't like you enough. It's possible that this person helps you keep this hope by not clarifying their feelings. Maybe you're not setting the right boundaries and playing the game because you're not sure what you want either, and this relationship helps you escape a life that doesn't fulfil you. Or maybe you just don't want to find out that this perfect, charming person is only human, and if you get to know them better you might end up disliking them. Feeling like you're absolutely destined to be together and that no other love could feel like this when you're not really committed to each other or experiencing true intimacy, is madness. You think they love you, but have they ever told you that? Have they proved it to you beyond all doubt?

I've often encountered women in my practice who ask me about a romance that's not yet materialized. They tell me how wonderful their relationship is, how they've never felt anything like it before and how incredibly close they are to this special person. They're convinced that this man is crazy about them, and they justify the fact the relationship hasn't progressed by claiming that he's afraid of commitment because he just got out of a relationship that caused him a lot of pain, poor guy! In the meantime, they sacrifice themselves by neglecting their true desires and emotional needs, and they never complain, lest they get hit by the harsh reality.

It's true that some people are "experts" in making us weak at the knees. They message you, you meet up, they treat you like a queen, you feel like the most special girl on the planet and then they disappear as if swallowed up by the earth. You might think, "how is that possible when everything was going so well! Something must have happened to them". Days go by and they call you again, tell you they miss you and you meet up again. They take you right back to cloud nine and then you're left hanging again, not understanding what's happening. You call them again one day, you arrange to meet and then they drop you again. In exchange for a night of good sex with you, they'll tell you some story about how special you are, that it's better this way, that this way the magic never ends... Whatever it takes to keep you available whenever they want you. You can't wait forever for them to acknowledge you so you can feel alive for a few hours. You have to be decisive and ask yourself what the relationship is really doing for you, because I assure you, it's doing absolutely nothing. Someone who's really interested in a woman doesn't mess around, they'll let you know. There are a lot more fish in the sea, my love, so don't waste your time.

Platonic love

Ah, platonic love... those sighs let out while looking at the sky, imagining what it would be like to be with that person. That little smile that has always mesmerized you, but then went away. That idyllic sensation that you felt in their presence that didn't stand the test of time. That unattainable love that's long been lost. Let me give you an example of a romance that sums this up perfectly.

Marta is a thirty-six-year-old woman. Eight years ago, at a beach resort, she signed up for surfing lessons. The instructor was a gorgeous, athletic, charming guy. He flirtatiously asked her out for a drink that evening. She was absolutely taken up with him but couldn't make the date because her friend fell ill and had to be taken to hospital. After that, she headed back to her country since it was the last day of her holiday, and she didn't see him again. Instead of letting the experience go, which would be the most normal thing to do, she never forgot about him. She got caught up in the "what ifs", to the point that years later she looked him up on social media and sent him a message. The guy, surprised, talked to her several times and they arranged to meet some day. He didn't remember her at all and didn't really have any intention of seeing her. He was just playing along or being polite – who knows. The fact is that she didn't see it that way; her imagination ran wild, and she started thinking that fate was intervening. There couldn't be any other explanation: life was giving them a second chance. She imagined herself getting married on that paradisiacal beach. She took a flight that same weekend to surprise him. When she landed in his city and messaged him, he didn't write back. You can imagine the look on this guy's face when he received a message from a girl he met once eight years ago, who'd just travelled across the ocean to meet him after they'd only spoken a couple of times. He probably freaked out. She'd magnified their encounter to stratospheric proportions. Imagine being in another country, alone, and receiving no reply from the person you thought you were meeting.

How far are our romantic fantasies capable of making us believe we're experiencing things that aren't actually happening? This reminds me of the online relationships where women spend months talking to men on the other side of the world. With nothing to on other than a photograph, they conjure up a romantic story for themselves even though they haven't yet shared a single day together. It makes me think of the Tinder swindler, a heartless, cruel guy who used social media to ensnare vulnerable victims, who he courted and seduced. He'd ask for money and then abandon them, leaving them in a state of shame and humiliation. These predators know how to select their victims. They target women who are lonely, desperate for romance, hypersensitive to heartbreak and have a low self-esteem. I can't help but see the hand of Neptune in these situations.

CLANDESTINE LOVE AFFAIRS

Love can take on a truly sad dimension if a woman with Venus in conjunction with Neptune ventures into a relationship with a man who's unavailable because he's with someone else. Although it's not the norm, adulterous relationships are more likely to occur between a married man and a single woman, although I repeat, I see a major shift in this trend in today's society. A man is capable of maintaining two significant relationships at the same time: one is the mother of his children, the woman who embodies the Moon, the one he's built a family with and the one who gives him emotional security and support. The other is Venus, the ideal woman who perfectly fulfils his erotic and romantic fantasies. The inability to find both archetypes in one woman may be one of the reasons why he seeks an extramarital relationship.

If no effort is made to maintain the spark, relationships eventually wear out and the desire to fulfil unsatisfied fantasies elsewhere sneaks in, though the individual wants to do this without foregoing the security of the familiar. The lover holds a deep hope that the object of her affections will leave his wife for her. She gets lost in the illusion of romance, and she simply can't fathom how the man who's madly in love with her doesn't want to share his life with her. So, there she stays, in a tremendously painful situation, hoping that one day he'll choose her, duped by the false promises and vain hopes. It can go on like this for years, because not being able to be with the loved one provokes very tense and powerful emotions, and these far outweigh what people feel in an ordinary relationship. Normally, they're the ones who end up breaking off the relationship, because they grow weary of the situation over time. If it is the man who breaks it off, the woman's self-image and self-esteem might be damaged for a much longer time.

LIBERATING WOMEN IN OUR LINEAGE

Neptune is the ruler of Pisces and the 12th house of the Zodiac. This planet is related to the collective unconscious and stores the memories of all the experiences lived by humanity. We're that drop that is lost in an infinite ocean, and each one of us possesses all the cellular memory of that vast body of water. These archetypal experiences are stored in the very deep unconscious that we can't access with our conscious mind. When Venus dips into the waters of that unconscious, the ancestral influence on our romantic experiences is very intense. The unhealed wounds that the women of our lineage experienced in love are very much alive within us, and they condition us greatly. We think we're living our own life, but there are traumatic experiences from the distant past that transcend time and space and are passed on from generation to generation. The experiences that our ancestors couldn't adequately resolve are our mission today. Frustrated romantic fantasies, traumas that were silenced, the terror they experienced, the pain they couldn't express... They're stored in our cells, in our womb, in the depths of our being.

Neptune leaves ajar a door that was meant to be closed, and this manifests as a faded memory, a nostalgia that lingers within us, a whisper of a distant voice. These deep ancestral memories lead us to long for particular romantic situations, to be fascinated by falling in love, to need to fulfil the frustrated dreams of the women who came before us. However, at the same time, we're afraid of love that we can't identify, and we're afraid of love when we don't know where it comes from. This is because the painful experiences they had are also stored in that deep memory. This can make us crave a beautiful connection, but not open ourselves to a committed relationship because a part of us feels that bad things will happen, even if we can't remember what exactly it is that we're afraid of. Our psyche needs to repeat unprocessed traumatic situations in order to heal them. So, we keep entering relationships that don't meet our expectations, and they leave us grieving, sad and deeply misunderstood. It's a never-ending cycle. These memories can manifest themselves in a very physical way, as a way of blocking our openness to sexual intercourse, such as vaginismus, dyspareunia, anorgasmia or uterine problems. For example, if one of our ancestors experienced sexual abuse, in this life we may experience difficulty in enjoying sexual intercourse in a way that can't be explained by anything we've experienced. The whole area at the top of the pelvic bone is our second energetic centre and is closely linked to Venus. It's there that we store the memories that come not only from our own experiences with love in this life, but also from our ancestral lineage. It possesses sexual energy, the power to create and the capacity to give and receive, to feel pleasure and be happy. Engaging in deep energetic healing in this area to release deep memories is good if you have Venus in the 12th house or in difficult aspect with Neptune.

Researching the experiences of women in the family and uncovering their stories can shed a lot of light on the circumstances you're living through. We're not alone in this; the women of our ancestral past are by our side supporting us in the process. They pass on the wisdom of their experience to us as long as we're open to listen. They know that we don't have the strength to free ourselves from this cycle, and that's why we've volunteered to stop being slaves to the archetype and be reborn into our own story. They want us to break out of the eternal illusion, the fantasy, the fairy tale, the dreams that swamp our lives and condition us. They push us to overcome our fears and experience true love, a love free of idealization, a love we can allow to grow with our feet firmly on the ground. When we're liberated, they are liberated too, enlightening our lineage.

EMBRACE THE MAGIC WITHOUT ESCAPING REALITY

A Neptunian will always look for that magic spark in their romantic connections. What mysterious force comes between two people who, without knowing each other at all, end up being in the same place at the same time and becoming helplessly attracted to each other? Love is fascinating. When you start to love someone, their minor flaws enchant you and make you feel a little weak at the knees. You love the person as they are, and you accept them wholly. But what if you try loving yourself in the same way – can you say out loud that you're completely worthy of love? To experience Neptune in a healthy way, you must love every part of yourself unconditionally.

We constantly compare ourselves to high expectations that we can't live up to. There's something inside us that tells us we're not good enough, not beautiful enough, not slim enough, not perfect enough. We live waiting for that special person to come riding in and tell us that we are enough, and to love us unconditionally. We place our happiness and all our hopes on the day when we can feel that way. While we wait, we despair, because there's nothing more important than being patient while we wait for that magical meeting.

It seems we can't be happy if we're not in a fantastic relationship. When we think this way, we're giving up our ability to create magic in every moment of our lives. You might be a hopeless romantic, but you rarely feel connected to nature, to your body, your cycles, your intuition or your ability to experience pleasure and enjoy the countless possibilities the world has to offer. See the love in your kitten's eyes; feel the magic of life in the tree in your garden, in a baby's tiny hands, in the sun that lights up your face. The love you're seeking is looking for you right now, and it will come to you when you're full of love and can inject it into everything you do. The path to love is never an external one: it's a journey within. When you honour your journey, when you find your path, you'll also find love. Neptune asks us to visit the spiritual essence of love, to unburden it of fantasies, to experience it in the here and now with every pore of our being. That source of inexhaustible creativity, inspiration, love and ecstasy is within you, you just have to peel back a few layers to access it. Always remember that, just by the fact of your existence, you are valuable and deeply loved.

CHAPTER 6

Pluto in relationships

The power of love

P

PLUTO IN
RELATIONSHIPS

You've always had the power, my dear.
THE WIZARD OF OZ

P luto is a transpersonal planet, a force that we can't control and which transcends us. It represents our soul's will to evolve. It's associated with death, perfection and power. It brings us intense, destructive and painful experiences, which provide us with the necessary catharsis to transform ourselves. The planet challenges us to reach our authentic potential in the most uncomfortable of ways.

The situations that are under Pluto's control leave us feeling powerless, as if we can't control anything and there are forces that transcend us. The master of the underworld is in charge of making us aware of everything that is hidden and unacknowledged in our psyche. Pluto takes us down to the depths of hell so that we can face our demons and everything we're unable to acknowledge. It's all there, boiling under the surface. The dark side of us, our unconscious desires, the impulses that dominate us, the things we repress, everything taboo, our shame: it all belongs to this planet's world, its realm. It mercilessly exposes all the pain, inexplicable fear, wounds, traumas and aspects in which we're most vulnerable. The more we resist, the more we try to control it, the more defiant it becomes, and we'll suffer for longer. It's relentless. It seeks unmitigated truth and authenticity. If something isn't right, Pluto will put it directly in front of you so you can face it. It takes a lot of courage to come clean about what we keep under lock and key, but there's more energy and real life in the things we're afraid of than in our comfort zone.

When we go through pain, and we accept and transform this darkness, we're reborn free, authentic and aligned with who we really are, revealing beautiful wings like a butterfly's that will allow us to fly high. Thanks to this transformation we can access hidden treasures, the most powerful, vibrant parts of us and all the potential that is yet to be awakened within us.

Pluto represents this principle of regeneration that drives life to shed its old forms and make way for new ones. It's the natural defence against stagnation. Everything is a cycle, everything has a start and an end, everything that rises reaches its highest point, and sooner or later it has to come back down. After happiness comes sadness; after success there's failure; after day there's night; after life comes death. Pretending to be constantly in the same state is an illusion: clinging to things is useless, because nothing can assume an eternal form. Pluto destroys the things we don't need, the things that have served their purpose and no longer helps us grow. It removes what no longer vibrates with us to make space for something new. We're beings who are constantly evolving, eternally transforming ourselves. We can't evolve if we don't break, if we don't hit rock bottom, if we don't let go.

Like a snake that sheds its skin, we must learn to accept this process unconditionally and be aware that we're not separate from the flow and rhythm of life.

Relationships are also subject to cycles and experience metamorphosis. First, we experience falling in love, where everything feels full and euphoric. Next comes the period of stability, which can vary in length. Then there's a moment of deception and crisis that can finish the relationship, but if this stage is overcome, the connection becomes stronger and the love becomes more authentic and true, free from idealization.

When Venus or the Moon are linked to Pluto, we can expect important challenges in our personal relationships. The main aspects to consider are the following:

★ Venus or the Moon in conjunction, opposition or square aspect with Pluto. These are aspects of tension and are depicted with a red line in your birth chart.

★ Pluto in the 1st, 4th or 7th house.

★ Venus or the Moon in Scorpio or the 8th house.

THE DARK GODDESSES

Many ancient goddesses were associated with Pluto's energy and worshipped, such as the black goddess Kali in India, Persephone in ancient Greece, Ereshkigal, Innana's sister and queen of the underworld, and Sekhmet in Egypt. These goddesses live in the shadows and represent archetypes that dwell deep within us. The goddess Kali rules darkness, death and regeneration. She's heir to the great goddess, the primordial and sacred feminine energy that pulsates throughout the universe, destructive and devouring, but also transformative and creative. Archetypically, she represents immortality, that which can't be destroyed and can only be transformed in an unending cycle of death and rebirth. She's depicted naked and dark, with loose, tousled hair, sharp fangs and a long, blood-stained tongue. Her nudity speaks to her wild nature, which is free from any restrictions. In one hand she holds a bloody scythe and in the other a severed human head. A necklace of skulls hangs around her neck. She speaks to us of the necessity of death and the false self, and encourages us to undergo an intense transformation that leads us to let go of everything we wrongly cling to. Her power destroys in order to create, and creates in order to uncreate, in an endless cycle. When we're open to giving things up, when we follow her lead, we can comprehend her mysteries. The goddess confronts us with what we fear the most, and when we pass through her inky darkness, she shows us the treasure that's hidden within. Her archetype leads us back to love, and to our authentic power and creativity. As an enlightened goddess, she shows us things as they really are: both what we can see and what we can't see. At some point in our lives, all of us begin the obligatory descent into the nether world. If we're only able to recognize the dark and destructive side of the feminine goddess, we'll be left confused, apathetic, empty and desperate for too long. We'll live in a black hole and look at life from the narrow mouth of our cave. However, if we're able to discover the ever-changing figure of the goddess and trust the process, the cave will open to reveal a bright light, even if we don't know where it leads.

Years ago, during a very special journey I took to Egypt, I discovered a goddess who fascinated me right from the very beginning. It was Sekhmet, the lion goddess, the divine and powerful mother who devoured us with her destructive and liberating fire. It's said that her breath created the desert. She's the lioness who scorches, burns and ravages everything that's not aligned with the truth. Her mission is to help us come clean about our destructive feelings and the animalistic rage we repress. The archetypal goddess roars within us, telling us, "your rage is part of your feminine power, don't reject it, make it your strongest ally." This loving mother destroys us so that we can be reborn and renewed, so that we can once again feel life's pulse beating within us.

STORMY RELATIONSHIPS

Complicated and turbulent relationships are a fact of life if we have Pluto influencing us in love. If a relationship is peaceful, we get bored. We want intensity, excitement and adrenaline. All or nothing, half measures don't mean anything to us. Love should be deep, unforgettable and transform us completely. The people who attract us give off an intense sexual magnetism, radiate power and security, and seem to have everything under control. But all too often, behind this impressive façade lies a psychologically damaged personality. Instinctively, we're pushed into impossible relationships or love triangles with problematic partners who are emotionally distant, in another relationship or suffer from an addiction of some sort. These relationships are complex and often come with a good dose of drama that's worthy of the silver screen, and we already know that mature, stable love has never been a big thing in the world of art. The most popular romances in both cinema and literature are stormy and full of passion, with insurmountable obstacles and fatal outcomes, always ending with a fiery reunion.

Romantic encounters influenced by Pluto have an intensity that's as beautiful as it is difficult to erase. Throughout our lives, many of us have experienced at least one romantic experience intense enough to leave us hooked. You've probably felt that inexplicable pull that sweeps you along like a huge wave pushing you to the bottom of the ocean. When you want to get out from underneath it, another wave rolls you back in and you sink even deeper. Some people come into our lives and touch the deepest parts of us, leaving a profound imprint on our soul. The first time you're with them you can't get them out of your mind. You feel a powerful desire for union, you want to feel them close again. You long to own the experience, to make it unalterable and indestructible. The memory is so vivid that it creates a wildly emotional state, and you swing between extremes of absolute happiness and overwhelming anxiety and restlessness. You can become so obsessed with that person that you often can't function in your own life; you completely lose focus and instead ride an emotional rollercoaster. You'll alternate between experiencing moments of absolute bliss and others of despondency and pain. One day you're in heaven, the next you're descending into the darkness of hell.

These relationships feature an intense passion of volcanic magnitude, and they're difficult to maintain over time. Both partners feel a powerful attraction and wish to fuse together, but at the same time, a part of them needs to step away so they can breathe; they know on an unconscious level that what they're feeling could destroy them. As such, both of them may feel that they need to control the situation in their own way, and their behaviour can sabotage the relationship. They find it easier to detach themselves from the partnership and go about their own business. We seem to be biologically and culturally programmed to fall into such destructive patterns.

Relationship addiction

If your partner becomes inaccessible and emotionally distant – perhaps they stop considering you important or distance themselves from you – you're left floating in the void, unable to understand what's going on. Drama soon ensues. All the coming and going, the obsession, the "can't live with you, can't live without you". A part of you knows this is bad and you need to get out, but you can't, because every time they reject you, you become more obsessed. You say to yourself that you'll never go back, but you do, excusing their behaviour over and over again. Who cares if they're driving you crazy; when you're back in their arms again, your world lights up. The truth is, you're not addicted to this person, you're addicted to the feeling of being with them. A part of you knows that the relationship wouldn't work if it became normal and stable. You resist breaking the pattern because you feel like you'll never know a love this strong again. But believe me, this is not love. Waiting around for someone who doesn't choose you, insisting on a person who can't be with you or give you what you deserve because they can't make up their own mind wears you down, and quickly. To stick around suffering and waiting for crumbs that get smaller and smaller each time in the vague hope that one day it will change, is something you don't deserve.

This type of love is an addiction and should be treated as such. Completely removing yourself from this type of relationship is like quitting a drug, and you might even experience the same emotional withdrawal symptoms, such as anxiety, nervousness, emotional discomfort, emptiness, despondency, depression and recurrent, obsessive thoughts. When you're no longer focused on the person who has been your outlet, there's no option but to take control of your own emotional world. Now you have the opportunity to heal your wounds and take the first steps towards a healthy sense of self-worth.

Relationships without attachments

Pluto teaches us a simple yet terrible truth: there's no such thing as "forever". The relationships characterized by this archetype are intentional and generate strong attachments. The people involved want to experience the relationship to the fullest, to the point of total exhaustion. The feelings can be so deep and extreme that they become all-consuming. There's a fear of losing that person, and this can generate a defensive and controlling attitude, which always ends up creating the thing the person fears the most. If you worry about the relationship changing or ending, you'll take on a possessive attitude that will cause the partnership to lose its magic. Every time we try to hold on to what we consider valuable, we end up dirtying it, because we become dependent. Without realizing it, we end up putting pressure on the person we love. Life is uncertain; when you meet someone new, there's no guarantee that it will work out. There's no tarot reader, astrologer, clairvoyant or oracle capable of assuring you that you'll grow old by their side. To maintain the relationship over time, you both need to come to an agreement: if there comes a time when you're no longer on the same page, you need to break things off without resistance. The beauty of remembering that it could end at any moment is that you give the best of yourselves every day and strive to please each other. It's as if every moment could be your last. This way no one feels pressured, because they're free to leave. If you're willing to give your partner this space, you're more likely to have a wonderful and long-lasting relationship.

Deep down we're all looking for someone who's not worried about the future of the relationship, instead affording us the room to breathe and letting the relationship develop organically. Detachment doesn't mean ceasing to feel, and it has nothing to do with being indifferent with a heart of stone. It's about opening yourself up completely, feeling everything and continuing onward. Fear takes the place of love and where there's fear there can be no love, so you need to remove fear from your relationship. Don't focus on possible outcomes, live in the here and now and enjoy every moment as if it's your last. Remember that love always conquers fear because it's so much more powerful.

Learning to let go

We cling to happiness when it crosses our path, and we want to hold on to it forever. We want to keep it, to own it, for everything to remain the same. However, we must understand that relationships go through phases. Happiness cannot be stored; people cannot be possessed. Real strength and true self-respect can only be achieved by learning to let go. We're constantly evolving, and therefore we must be willing to let go of what no longer vibrates with us, what holds us back and keeps us stagnated. When you enter into a relationship with someone, it's perfect for you at that time in your life, but there may come a day when you want to grow and develop your potential, and the other person is not so willing. Then the relationship becomes unbalanced. It's as if you're on different trains: one of you on a high-speed train and the other on a stopping service. If you continue to stay in a relationship that has run its course, the only thing you'll achieve is toxicity or, at the very least, dissatisfaction. The partnership will deteriorate, like a swamp of stagnant water full of mould, insects, bacteria and waste with a putrid smell. Because the water can't circulate, life can't be renewed. Every day, you need to decide what's good for you: if a relationship no longer supports your growth, it's time to let it go. When you let go, you discover something magical... All the energy that was trapped in your relationship is now available for a new love that's more in tune with you.

Being honest about your dark side

We all have a dark side, a hidden side to our personality that's totally unknown to us but others can recognize. In a relationship, it's not uncommon for us to be criticized for these attitudes, leaving us surprised since we're not able to see ourselves reflected in them. However, the more we repress these parts of us, the more apparent they become to our partner. Paradoxically, the things we don't recognize about ourselves are the things that wind us up when we see them in other people. This is known as projection, a defence mechanism through which we attribute our own shortcomings, feelings, impulses, desires and character flaws that we don't acknowledge because we find them unacceptable to someone else. Pluto shows us parts of ourselves that we've hidden under lock and key through relationships, and it's important to free them so that we can become everything we can be. The more perfect and kind we believe ourselves to be, the more destructive our dark side; conversely, if we dare to let our personality show some of that "lesser" nature, the more balanced our life will be and the freer we will feel. By integrating our dark side, we perform a type of alchemy, transforming the darkest of things into higher vibrational energy. We've been taught to fear our dark side, but so much of our strength lies within it. For generations, we've been forced to repress the instinctive, unacceptable and destructive parts of us, but daring to open up and express them wisely will return us to our power.

Be authentic

When we grow, we shape a personality that we consider appropriate to be integrated into the social environment. Paradoxically, in Plutonian family structures we over-adapt to the nuclear family – that is, the family functions as a clan that has the power to give us all the affection and protection we need. However, belonging to that group comes at a price,and that is foregoing the desire to function as a totally independent person.When we're young, we feel it necessary to hide impulses and behaviours that aren't appropriate to gain approval, containing a lot of our innate energy and curiosity as a consequence. Because of our need for love and protection, we sacrifice our truest nature. This is most palpable when Pluto is in conjunction with the Moon, and we can spend our lives torn between our need for freedom and loyalty to our family values. Daring to be who we are, even if it goes against what's expected of us, takes bravery. However, it's incredibly liberating to break through the guilt and summon the courage to live our lives as we truly want to.

VICTIM AND PERPETRATOR: TWO SIDES OF THE SAME COIN

The victim and the perpetrator are archetypal positions strongly related to Pluto. A Plutonian person might unconsciously make themselves a perpetrator and control and dominate their partner, or they might place themselves in the position of a victim. These positions are two sides of the same coin, two extreme manifestations of the same energy. It's important to clarify that the essence of the planet and what it asks of us is one thing, and how each of us translates and uses that energy is quite another. That is dependent on many factors such as our level of personal development, and this is where the archetypes come into play. They are a concept coined by Carl Gustav Jung, who referred to a "pattern of the psyche", which does its best to defend itself against the intensity of the energy of the transpersonal planets – normally unconsciously. These patterns are activated according to personal experiences that have left an intense "imprint" on our souls, such as significant childhood experiences. The victim is an archetypal position developed for pure survival, a "resource" that we use when we feel powerless and overwhelmed by our circumstances and believe that we're unable to change them.

There can be painful events that push us past our breaking point, situations such as being a victim of abuse who's unable to react. In these cases, it's common for the victim archetype to flourish. However, generally speaking, we have two options: we can stay stuck in our eternal suffering or confront our situation with dignity. We become victims when we constantly complain but never do anything to bring about change. "Why do all the bad things always happen to me? I'm so unlucky, the world is so unfair and life is terrible. I always attract difficult men; I can't trust anyone..." If we always consider ourselves the "good guy" and everyone else the "bad guy", we're unconsciously seeking pity and victimizing ourselves. This attitude is a way of avoiding our responsibility for the situations we find ourselves in and blaming fate for all the catastrophes and misfortunes that come our way. Who can say that they've never blamed someone else for their unhappiness? When we do this, we're giving up all our power and, as goddesses, we cannot afford to do that.

If we maintain this constant feeling of disempowerment, we'll develop a sense of inferiority because we're unaware of our inner resources and true strength. Consequently, it will be easy to fall into difficult relationships in which we unconsciously give up power and unwittingly become subjugated, emotionally dependent and vulnerable.

Plutonian women are more likely to play the role of victim within a relationship, because biologically and culturally we're programmed to please, love, adapt, protect and comfort – although, of course, this is not the rule. Often a woman gives up her desires (Venus) or emotional needs (Moon) and complies with her partner's demands. If she repeats this behaviour without setting appropriate boundaries, it will probably be too late when she tries to rebel, and conflict will ensue. In this way, she'll gradually place herself in a position of subjugation and will cede all power to her partner, who will be able to get everything they want and need from her. The victim gives herself to her partner completely, sacrificing herself to prevent them from abandoning her. She submits herself because she depends on the other person, believing she needs them to feel happy.

Many of these relationships are structured as a result of living in a combative environment. It's normal for a child to fear a lack of parental control if they've grown up in a dysfunctional family alongside addiction, violence, abuse, fighting or instability. The home, which is supposed to provide love and protection, is instead experienced as a source of threat and conflict. Faced with this profound helplessness, a strong survival instinct develops. These experiences are overwhelming and devastating and leave a strong emotional scar on the psyche. Confronted with its powerlessness, the child will probably go on to develop relationships that involve power games and manipulative behaviours that perpetuate inequality. Instances of emotional abuse will be frequent; for example, a woman might use sex to control the man and get what she wants, an individual might use silence or indifference to punish their partner, or a man might emotionally abuse his partner before coming back and using a Prince Charming act to ask for forgiveness.

Next to the victim is the person who seems to dominate the relationship. Feeling strong and useful to their partner helps them feel in control, because unconsciously they're terrified of experiencing the panic and helplessness they knew in the past. The perpetrator is Mr or Mrs Perfect, possessing only positive attributes, while the other person has only mistakes and flaws. Any problem that crops up in the relationship is never their fault. They might occasionally speak with an aggressive tone, and will regularly try to lay down the law. Unconsciously, they want the connection with their partner to be indestructible, everlasting and so unalterable that nothing can change it. They're terrified that the relationship will break down because they know deep down that they would be devastated, so they make sure their partner helps them to keep their emotions intact. The perpetrator fears being dependent and is terrified of the possibility of revisiting the feelings of abandonment they experienced in childhood. The object of their affection has to be completely predictable, and as soon as they detect the slightest bit of distance, they become demanding. This person is distrustful and fears betrayal. Since no relationship can stay the same forever, they feel jealous and are overcome with the need to possess their partner as if they were their property when they get the slightest inkling that the other person is becoming distant. The perpetrator feels powerless and considers themselves inferior. The only way they can feel in control is by minimizing and manipulating their partner. What they fear most is they won't be accepted for who they really are, and they'll use any manipulative and emotionally abusive technique to undermine their partner's self-confidence and make them believe they couldn't cope without them.

As you've likely already noticed, both these positions are intertwined and share the same symptoms. Both are dependent, both feel powerless and inferior, and both have low self-esteem. The victim will try to change their partner, but they won't succeed. People don't change unless they work on themselves deeply. It's very difficult for the perpetrator to stop this behaviour because it benefits them; it's their way of avoiding their own dark side. The perpetrator is the great master who confronts this shadow with their own power again and again.

ANALYZING THE REST OF THE BIRTH CHART

As you can see, in any relation influenced by Pluto there's a good dose of emotional intensity and attraction, but there are levels to it that depend on various factors such as family environment, self-esteem and the society we live in. On an astrological level, it also depends on other aspects that are dependent on Venus and the Moon. Because of this, it's important to analyze the birth chart in its entirety, because we are the sum of lots of different energies. For example, if the Moon or Venus are aspected with Saturn, this will create a different experience; there will be more opportunities to impose limitations and regulate the dramatic intensity, or else we'll stay single for a long time because of our fear of suffering. If Uranus enters into the equation, we'll either be more capable of detaching ourselves and viewing everything with a more emotional distance, or we'll more readily fall into on-and-off relationships that cause us pain. If Neptune is involved, the results can be even more complex and terrible because the concept of romantic love will be put on a pedestal. We already know that idealizing the other person doesn't help us see the reality and the dynamics of the relationship clearly. Throw in the Neptunian concepts of dedication and sacrifice and it becomes more difficult to let go of this toxic bond.

RESENTMENT AND GUILT

We've all experienced a relationship in which we didn't value ourselves and gave in time and again for very little in return. No matter how competent and capable we may have been in other areas of life, in that relationship we were but children hungry for love and appreciation. When we let go of these toxic relationships, we're filled with uncomfortable feelings of guilt for not knowing how to get out of the relationship and for having put up with behaviour that we didn't deserve. When we stay in an abusive relationship for too long without setting appropriate boundaries, we're left tremendously vulnerable. If we've been humiliated or deeply hurt, we can become ensconced in hatred, anger and resentment. To feel empowered again, we might plot revenge as a way of defending ourselves against humiliation, betrayal or rejection. A lot of revenge may have an element of poetic justice and feel particularly liberating and cathartic. It's true that there are some people who deserve our turning the wind into a storm and hurling it straight at them, but being above those destructive emotions is especially healing and helps us avoid becoming the very thing that's hurt us so much: the persecutor.

HEALING OUR WOUNDS

Although most parents do the best they can, they can never fill the emptiness we carry within us. It never feels like enough because the fusion between us and our parents can't match the fusion with the primordial source we came from. The moment we're born, we experience our first wound, being separated from the infinite ocean of love we belong to. We're left with deep feelings of abandonment and rejection that accompany us throughout our lives, which we can't allow ourselves to feel. We blame our parents for not having known how to remedy this isolation and sense of separation. On top of that, we live in a world where we're constantly confronted with difficult situations and challenging experiences that leave their mark on us. In order to heal our wounds, there are no shortcuts. We must learn to let them hurt, burn and sting until the pain stops. Any addiction, whether it's to food, substances or toxic relationships, is masking a deep, unacknowledged emotional pain. We have truly original mechanisms for escaping pain. As women, we've been brought up to be strong and carry more than our fair share of life's burdens. We must learn to let go of the dead weight and free ourselves from the heavy emotions and negative energy that prevents us from breezing through life.

You can't control or tame your emotions. They surge into your consciousness in waves, and we need to learn to surf them. If we ignore them, they'll grow bigger and wash us away. Let them flow freely, feel them in all their intensity and then let go. Surrender to them. Don't control them. Don't avoid them. When we come out of our mother's womb, we scream and cry at the top of our lungs. We instinctively express what we naturally feel; we don't go to the fridge for a piece of chocolate. Resisting reality generates frustration, so allow yourself to feel your fears, your sadness, even your confusion. If you're feeling low, let yourself feel that emotion until a different one comes along. Breathe, go with the flow, let go... Above all, let go.

A GODDESS ALWAYS KNOWS HOW TO RESTORE HER POWER

There's immense power and creativity within you. You have enormous potential that's just waiting for you to wake up and recognize its presence. You're free to walk away from that strength if you want. You can lose yourself in the world, tormented by doubt, apathy and confusion, unaware of all the treasures you possess, but that energy will lovingly push you back to that deep part of yourself. You've been carrying that existential emptiness and constant dissatisfaction for too long. You can feel something inside you, a whisper telling you that your life is valuable and that you're here to do so much more. And so you start your quest to return to the parts of yourself that you've forgotten, to once again know who you really are, to restore your power. Conquering that place of authentic empowerment overrides the tendency to give into victimhood, feeling powerless, falling into despair and losing motivation. That inner strength helps you captain your own ship, to be the master of your own life and to navigate it with courage, without ever being discouraged, knowing that there's a compass guiding your steps. This vibration is full of vitality, inexhaustible inspiration, true love and confidence. It pushes you to find what you love and to develop your unique talents.

When you start exploring the things you like and define a goal, you become immune to addiction and deeply respect yourself. You no longer stay stagnating in relationships that don't bring anything positive into your life; you don't need drama and intensity to feel that the relationship is alive. You still love passionately, but you also offer security and peace. You radiate the idea that you'd be perfectly fine on your own, the sort of energy that's not suitable for insecure guys. Poison no longer seems that attractive to you. You know how to detect the power games that are indicative of a hidden fear of intimacy. You never, under any circumstances, allow yourself to be manipulated. You always enjoy life, embrace your emotions and dance with your dreams. You've returned to your intuitive knowledge, your ancient wisdom, your power, which is beyond anything else on this Earth. Once you remember who you are, you'll never want to lose yourself again.

THE TRANSFORMATION

Relationships that bear the stamp of Pluto take us down to rock bottom. We descend down into hell and face our demons. Once we manage to get out of it, we're left to pick ourselves up and put ourselves back together. These bonds become catalysts for the radical transformation we need to return to our power. They're the great teachers that point to the parts of us that are incomplete and show us all the love we weren't giving ourselves. Only when we expose ourselves to that destruction can we reach the bits of us that are indestructible. When we travel through the darkness we emerge wiser, liberated and whole. This doesn't mean you'll no longer experience a passionate relationship – of course you will – but it won't be toxic. You can both experience a very deep connection and bullet-proof love. The type of love where you can always be yourself and help each other heal your emotional wounds. Above all, you'll have the opportunity to help increase each other's potential. This is the immense gift that this planet offers you.

CHAPTER 7

The axis of relationships

The power of love

THE AXIS OF RELATIONSHIPS

Normally, we say something along the lines of, "I'm an Aries" when we're talking about our star sign, but this only refers to the position of the Sun in our birth chart. It's common for us to easily identify with the attributes of our Sun sign since the Sun represents the conscious side of our personality. Most of the sign compatibilities we find in magazines or online also refer to the Sun sign. This represents a very small part of who we are in terms of energy, as our birth chart is a much more complex and nuanced structure. One of the key elements to consider when it comes to understanding the dynamics of personal relationships is the ascendant–descendant axis.

The sign that rises above the eastern horizon at the time of your birth corresponds to the ascendant (AC). This sign has a decisive influence on your personality. It represents the face you show to the world, how you're perceived by others and it reflects your physical characteristics. It's also the energy you need to develop and perfect throughout your life. When you meet a person for the first time, this sign affects your first impressions of them.

The energy of the ascendant is, in principle, subconscious. Through life's experiences, it helps us gradually identify with what we "are". The less we recognize ourselves in this sign, the more we project these traits onto others. We then attract people who embody this energy and mirror back to us what we're unable to see in ourselves. When I refer to a person who embodies the energy of a sign, in my experience it's usually a person with the Sun in that sign, because they express those qualities in a clear and conscious way. For example, if a woman doesn't identify with her Taurus ascendant, she may be attracted to and fall in love with a guy whose Sun is in Taurus. This guy will embody the qualities of this sign, and some will fascinate her and others will repel her. This is nothing more than a psychic reaction to her own unrecognized energy. This type of coupling occurs very frequently.

The descendant (DC) is the opposite point from the ascendant, and it's located on the cusp of the 7th house, which is the field of expertise associated with relationships. The ascendant represents the qualities we look for in a partner and the energy that complements ours. If the ascendant represents "what I am", then the opposite sign represents "what I am not" and reflects qualities that we don't recognize as our own. Whatever our consciousness doesn't recognize is projected onto and experienced through another person. For example, if we have an ascendant in Libra, we'll be incredibly attracted to a Sun person or someone with their ascendant in Aries – which is the opposite sign. This person will be very active and individualistic and will force us to develop and demand the Libran qualities of equality and balance. It'll be a creative relationship since it will enhance the qualities of our ascendant.

In the image below, we see a woman whose ascendant is Virgo and descendant is Pisces. The Moon is in Taurus and the 9th house, and her Sun is in Aries and the 8th house.

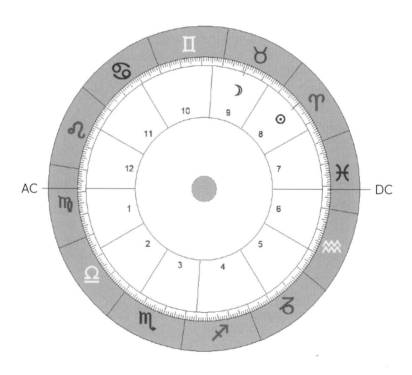

In short, opposites transform each other and help each other grow. They are necessary teachers who encourage us to integrate the things we find hardest to bring out. That person will make us feel as if we're being given something that we lack, and it's up to us to ensure that this doesn't end in confrontation and that it's an enriching experience. We can't properly develop the ascendant's energy without also integrating the opposite energy. This is why a relationship represents an important opportunity to discover ourselves and evolve.

Magnetic attraction between opposites is nothing new; we often see couples whose signs are opposite each other on the zodiacal wheel. Opposites interact and learn through contrast. There are always two sides to every story and for every light there is a darkness. When we turn on a light, we immediately see a shadow.

However, these opposite individuals are essentially compatible. They have the similar basic motivations (cardinal, fixed and mutable) and they correspond to compatible elements (fire and air; earth and water). Nonetheless, they're different enough to keep the spark alive for as long as possible.

Below, I briefly describe the 12 ascendants and their complementary opposites so that you can understand how both signs can mutually support and nourish each other. These interpretations correspond to the axis of relationships – that is to say, the signs situated on the ascendant and the descendant, but you can also apply them to your Sun sign if you wish.

♈ ARIES–LIBRA ♎

If you were born with your ascendant in Aries, you're a warrior woman. Ever since you were a little girl, life has pushed you to do things on your own, without anybody's help. You're a born leader and have an entrepreneurial spirit. You're not afraid of adventure and you know better than anybody when to take the initiative and make decisions. You know what you want, and you're bold enough to go for it. The problem is that you often do things your own way and focus too much on yourself, not taking others into account. You'd be complemented by a Libran who knows how to win you over and shower you with attention, but also teaches you by example how to relate, listen to and empathize with others. In order to create something new, you'll need to know that actions have repercussions. You'll learn that your desires can't be independent from your surroundings and that words and actions sometimes have consequences. Through your partner you'll discover that, the more open you are to sharing, the more you'll find out what you really want.

♎ LIBRA–ARIES ♈

If you're a Libra ascendant, you embody elegance and grace. You have a talent for creating social connections, diplomacy and art. You know how to empathize and can easily put yourself in another person's shoes, understanding them, listening to them and understanding their points of view – even if they're different to yours. However, your indecision is a thing of legend, and this is a daily struggle for you. Every time you have to take the initiative, you carefully weigh up the pros and cons, and doubt can paralyze you. This is why you're compatible with Aries, since people with this sign are great at making quick, spontaneous decisions. In this relationship, you'll gradually come to learn that this quality that you admire so much in your partner is also within you. With time, you'll become more independent from your surroundings, and you'll get used to relying on your own desires and taking risks without considering anyone else's opinion. When you try to impose your will, you'll round out your personality and be able to establish necessary boundaries.

♉ TAURUS–SCORPIO ♏

Being born with an ascendant in a Venus-ruled sign makes you some-one who emanates beauty and sensuality. Life teaches you to be patient, that things take time. You seek stability and you can stay in some situations longer than you should. You're peaceful and don't over-complicate life and you value tranquillity more than anything. You hate drama and conflict, but ooh la la... on the opposite side is Scorpio. You're fascinated by their dark side and their intense, passionate emotions. They never let anything go and are always ready to bring the parts of the relationship that aren't working to light, even if you don't like it. On the other hand, they help you avoid stagnation and let go of what doesn't benefit you so that you can make room for new experiences. Through them, you'll learn that things are constantly changing, that after a period of stability comes a period of transformation. Here, sexuality and sensuality come together, and it sends sparks flying!

♏ SCORPIO–TAURUS ♉

If you were born with an ascendant in the sign of Scorpio, you've had to learn tough and complicated lessons. You've had no choice but to learn to let things go, and you're all too familiar with emotional pain. You're enigmatic and magnetic, and sometimes you give the impression that you're hiding something. You're indestructibly headstrong and can face the worst situations and come out stronger and renewed. Taurus doesn't pass you by unnoticed; you're attracted to their peaceful way of dealing with life. They never get upset about anything and know how to weather any storm. You tend to be distrustful and go to extremes, which can lead to jealousy. They will teach you to tone down your intensity, to relax and enjoy the present. Things take time to mature, you don't need to be constantly changing everything. Just enjoy being alive and all the gifts life has to offer you, and they'll show you a world of pleasure and sensuality. Enjoy it!

♊ GEMINI–SAGITTARIUS ♐

With a Gemini ascendant, you have a great ability to socialize and relate to the whole of existence, without leaving anybody out. You walk through life with a curious spirit and a curious soul. Versatility is one of your gifts and you adapt wonderfully to any change that life throws your way. Your smile is contagious, and you always bring fun and happiness with you wherever you go. The problem is that you have too many interests, so it's difficult for you to master one thing in particular. You like to have a go at everything, and when you're immersed in something, it's easy to distract you and lead you off course. A partner with a Sagittarius sign will help you concentrate and focus your energy on one thing. They know how to guide you and encourage you to give that one thing your all. Furthermore, they'll show you that there are things that defy logic, and you'll be infected by their broad and transcendent take on life. You both share a love of freedom and learning new things, so this can be a very enriching relationship.

♐ SAGITTARIUS–GEMINI ♊

With the Sagittarian energy you radiate, you have the gift of inspiring others and you possess an unbelievable power of persuasion. Life will lead you to search for a purpose that gives your existence meaning. You always focus on the bright side, you're driven by your intuition and incredible optimism and you'll set your sights on new goals with a surplus of confidence. Gemini will help you understand that things are more complex than they seem and that it's good to analyze the practical details of every situation. They'll teach you that having doubts is sometimes necessary and will help you avoid a lot of disappointment. When you believe in something you do it with unshakeable faith; you have your truth and your ideals, and it's difficult for anyone to change them. Gemini will show you different places and open you to new experiences and points of view. Through their example, you'll see that absolute truths don't exist – not everything is black and white, and there are many ways of perceiving the same reality. They'll help you see new and exciting options that you'd previously overlooked and there's no way you'll ever get bored with each other.

♋ CANCER–CAPRICORN ♑

If you were born with your ascendant in the sign of the crab, you're a sensitive soul who exudes a warm and welcoming femininity. You're often guided to act according to how you're feeling in that moment, although you know how to love intelligently. You're protective and have a natural maternal instinct. You love being surrounded by "your people" and enjoy a quiet, homely, family-orientated life. You can show the world your tough side, but inside you have a vulnerable heart. You tend to stick to specific people, like a crab that grabs something with its claws and won't let go. You're attracted to Capricorns because they offer you stability and protection. With their loyalty and ambition, they teach you to be strong, set yourself goals and be independent. Following their example, you can learn how to leave the warmth of your comfort zone and venture off to conquer lands where your loved ones can't protect you. You'll discover that love is not synonymous with dependency and that you can love someone without becoming a part of them.

♑ CAPRICORN–CANCER ♋

Having a Capricorn ascendant endows you with power and strong will. Ever since you were young, you've known that life doesn't give you anything, you have to make the effort. Even then, things will take their time – you can't rush things. You have an uncanny ability to plan your future, and you know what steps to take and how much time you need to get where you want to go. Life has taught you that most dreams don't come true on their own; they need your discipline, commitment and dedication. Cancers are irresistible to you. Those gentle eyes are able to melt your cold heart. You work perfectly together, and they bring you that homely warmth you need after you've been striving for your professional goals. You'll feel completely content with them, and their embrace comforts you like nothing you've ever known. They teach you that feeling your emotions isn't something to fear, and that love isn't a waste of time – quite the opposite. Having a strong emotional foundation will help you navigate the world in a more mature way.

♌ LEO–AQUARIUS ♒

If your ascendant falls in the sign of the Sun, you have the essence of a diva and know how to let your own light shine. You need to do creative things, show them to the world and have them recognized. If this doesn't happen, you can become deeply unsatisfied. Your demeanour is unusually strong and dignified, and you inject your enthusiasm and vibrancy into the people who surround you. When you pick up the microphone, you don't let it go and this can cause you some problems with others who also want to say their piece. Then along comes Aquarius with their free, unattached aura, and they win you over. While your identity feels very set, they flee from all labels. They'll encourage you to be different no matter what people think. With them, you don't take things personally and can relate to your friends as part of the group, working together for a common interest. In time you'll realize that when you don't seek the limelight, you're a natural leader and become the centre of attention.

≈ AQUARIUS–LEO ♌

As an Aquarius ascendant, you know first-hand that change is the only constant in this universe – not that that thrills you. You have a touch of rebelliousness about you that makes you unique, and you're not shy about expressing the opinions that are formed deep within you – even if they go against what the majority think. Looking at things from a substantial distance helps you maintain an objective outlook that's emotionally detached from what's happening. Even though you might not know it sometimes, you're a free spirit and you need your own space where no one can control or condition you. You express yourself with originality, do unusual things and enjoy dressing in a way that goes against the norm. You love Leos because of their passion and how they put their heart into everything they do. They're not afraid of commitment and offer you unconditional loyalty. They're brave and tough; a born leader who knows how to steer their ship and achieve what they set out to do. They'll teach you to get off the fence, get involved, be passionate and stop running away from labels. You'll discover that beyond your solid idealism and the causes you fight for, you also need to leave your own mark on the world and work towards your personal goals. Together, you form a partnership with incredible creative potential. Make the most of it!

♍ **VIRGO–PISCES** ♓

As a Virgo ascendant, you're naturally serious and reserved. You give off an aura of intelligence, probably because you love to focus on the detail and nuance of any discipline you undertake. You're an extreme perfectionist, and you have to do everything perfectly. You're always searching for logical and rational explanations for everything. You're very sensitive to any bodily discomfort and anything beyond your control makes you nervous. You fall in love with Pisces' magical sensitivity and bohemian style. With them, you experience what it means to go with the flow and let life take you where it wants to. You'll come to learn that control is an illusion and that you don't always need to think about and understand everything, you just need to breathe and feel the moment. The key is to remember that not everything is what it seems, and there's much more to life than what we can experience with our physical senses. Maybe you should both join a yoga class!

♓ **PISCES–VIRGO** ♍

As a Pisces ascendant, you're endowed with extreme sensitivity and receptivity. This means that everything affects and alters you, and sometimes you need to shut yourself off from the outside world. You're a perceptive soul who is in touch with all of life's nuances and subtleties. You can sometimes find reality too tough, and you tend to seek refuge in your incredible imagination. You're very intuitive, but sometimes you don't trust your inner voice. You need to learn to establish boundaries so that others don't take advantage of you. Virgo is your perfect match. This intelligent, down-to-earth person knows how to give you the reassurance you need. They possess the necessary rationality to bring you back down to earth when you get lost in your own world or in the middle of some emotional turmoil. They believe in you and give you the push you need to leave your little bubble and start working on your dreams. They know that to bring out your full creative potential you need to discipline yourself and concentrate on the practical details. Only then will you be able to bring order to your chaos.

Afterword

We've come to the end of this book, and I hope that the journey has been enriching for you. The fact you've read it is no coincidence; it means that the search for something deeper and the need to reconnect with the wisdom of the powerful woman you are has been awakened within you, and that makes me very happy.

When writing this book, my greatest wish was to provide you with useful tools and valuable resources to guide you in your relationships. If I've also been able to convey my love for the wonderful art of astrology and you've seen yourself reflected in some of my words, I will have certainly fulfilled my heart's desires. I don't see how there can be love between a couple if there's not first a radical love for oneself, and this is one of the fundamental pillars that I've tried to express. Maybe this journey we've been on together won't end here, and we can meet again somewhere down the road.

Always be yourself and never stop shining.

Remember that you're worthy of all the love in the world.

Thank you for your light.

Acknowledgements

My heartfelt thanks go to my brother Lázaro for using the right words when I needed them most and for encouraging me to write. Thanks for helping me believe in myself and to understand the value of hard work.

To my partner, for being there to encourage and support me. You definitely came into my life at exactly the right time.

To all my family… To my parents, my brother Nacho and my daughter Ángela for your patience.

To my friends, the wonderful souls and powerful sorceresses who accompany me through life's journey.

To Berta and Eugenia, my Spanish publishers, for having faith in me and giving me total freedom to write.

To all the incredible women who follow me online, who are always there with their kind words to give me all the strength I need.

And, of course, thank you to the universe for the opportunity. Life can be incredibly magical.

Books that inspired me

Baring, Anne, and Cashford, Jules, *The Myth of the Goddess*, Penguin, 1993.

Bolen, Jean Shinoda, *Goddesses in Everywoman*, Harper, 2014.

Dickson, Elinor, and Woodman, Marion, *Dancing in the Flames: The Dark Goddess in the Transformation of Consciousness*, Shambhala, 1997.

Federichi, Silvia, *Caliban and the Witch*, Penguin Classics, 2021.

Frazer, James, *The Golden Bough*, OUP Oxford, 2009.

Gimbutas, Marija, *The Language of the Goddess*, Thames and Hudson, 2001.

Graves, Robert, *The Greek Myths*, Penguin, 2017.

Greene, Liz, *Saturn: A New Look at an Old Devil*, Weiser Books, 2011

ibid., *The Art of Stealing Fire: Uranus in the Horoscope*, CPA Press, 2004.

Greene, Liz, and Sasportas, Howard, Luminaries, Red Wheel/Weiser, 1992.

ibid., *Inner Planets*, Weiser, 1993.

Jung, Carl Gustav, *The Archetypes and the Collective Unconscious*, Routledge, 1991.

Mohanty, Seema, *Book of Kali*, Penguin Books India, 2009.

Moore, Patrick, *The Planet Venus*, Faber and Faber, 1956.

Northrup, Christiane, *Women's Bodies, Women's Wisdom*, Piatkus, 2009.

Pinkola Estés, Clarissa, *Women who Run with the Wolves*, Rider, 2008.

Sasportas, Howard, *The Twelve Houses*, Flare Publications, 2007.

Tompkins, Sue, *Aspects in Astrology*, Rider, 2001.